GALLUP YOUTH SURVEY: MAJOR ISSUES AND TRENDS

TEENS & SUICIDE

Hal Marcovitz

Developed in Association with the Gallup Organization

GALLUP YOUTH SURVEY: MAJOR ISSUES AND TRENDS

TEENS & SUICIDE

Hal Marcovitz

Developed in Association with the Gallup Organization

Mason Crest
450 Parkway Drive, Suite D
Broomall, PA 19008
www.masoncrest.com

© 2014 by Mason Crest, an imprint of National Highlights, Inc.

Printed and bound in the United States of America.

CPSIA Compliance Information: Batch #GYS2013. For further information, contact Mason Crest at 1-866-MCP-Book

First printing
1 3 5 7 9 8 6 4 2

Library of Congress Cataloging-in-Publication Data

Marcovitz, Hal.
  Teens and suicide / Hal Marcovitz.
    pages cm. — (The Gallup youth survey : major issues and trends)
  Includes bibliographical references and index.
  Audience: Grade 7 to 8.
  ISBN 978-1-4222-2958-3 (hc)
  ISBN 978-1-4222-2995-8 (pb)
  ISBN 978-1-4222-8875-7 (ebook)
  1. Teenagers—Suicidal behavior—Juvenile literature. 2. Suicide—Juvenile literature. 3. Depression in adolescence—United States—Juvenile literature. I. Title.
  HV6546.M35 2014
  362.280835'0973—dc23
                        2013007181

The Gallup Youth Survey: Major Issues and Trends series ISBN: 978-1-4222-2948-4

Contents

Introduction

By George Gallup

As the United States moves into the new century, there is a vital need for insight into what it means to be a young person in America. Today's teenagers will be the leaders and shapers of the 21st century. The future direction of the United States is being determined now in their hearts and minds and actions. Yet how much do we as a society know about this important segment of the U.S. populace who have the potential to lift our nation to new levels of achievement and social health?

We need to hear the voices of young people, and to help them better articulate their fears and their hopes. Our youth have much to share with their elders—is the older generation really listening? Is it carefully monitoring the hopes and fears of teenagers today? Failure to do so could result in severe social consequences.

The Gallup Youth Survey was conducted between 1977 and 2006 to help society meet this responsibility to youth, as well as to inform and guide our leaders by probing the social and economic attitudes and behaviors of young people. With theories abounding about the views, lifestyles, and values of adolescents, the Gallup Youth Survey, through regular scientific measurements of teens themselves, served as a sort of reality check.

Surveys reveal that the image of teens in the United States today is a negative one. Teens are frequently maligned, misunderstood, or simply ignored by their elders. Yet over four decades the Gallup Youth Survey provided ample evidence of the very special qualities of the nation's youngsters. In fact, if our society is less racist, less sexist, less polluted, and more peace loving, we can in considerable measure thank our young people, who have been on the leading edge on these issues. And the younger generation is not geared to greed: survey after survey has shown that teens have a keen interest in helping those people, especially in their own communities, who are less fortunate than themselves

Young people have told Gallup that they are enthusiastic about helping others, and are willing to work for world peace and a healthy world. They feel positive about their schools and even more positive about their teachers. A large majority of American teenagers have reported that they are happy and excited about the future, feel very close to their families, are likely to marry, want to have children, are satisfied with their personal lives, and desire to reach the top of their chosen careers.

But young adults face many threats, so parents, guardians, and concerned adults must commit themselves to do everything possible to help tomorrow's parents, citizens, and leaders avoid or overcome risky behaviors so that they can move into the future with greater hope and understanding.

The Gallup Organization is enthusiastic about this partnership with Mason Crest Publishers. Through carefully and clearly written books on a variety of vital topics dealing with teens, Gallup Youth Survey statistics are presented in a way that gives new depth and meaning to the data. The focus of these books is a practical one—to provide readers with the statistics and solid information that they need to understand and to deal with each important topic.

— — —

Teen suicide is a growing problem in the United States. As many as one-fifth of teens today have considered or attempted suicide. Tragically, thousands of U.S. teens actually commit suicide each year.

Parents who have experienced a child's suicide may remain haunted by questions about why a child took his or her life, and if there was something that could have been done to prevent it. This book, I believe, will bring about a new level of understanding of this unsettling issue. In both adults and teens, suicide often results from overwhelming feelings of rejection, abandonment, fear, or a sense of loss. Parents need to take seriously teen despondence, because it can lead to suicide.

A healthy family habit would be for parents to set aside a little time each day—perhaps at dinner or bedtime—and ask their children, "How did things go today?" Parents should then then listen carefully, and follow the discussion with a hug and the words, "I love you." Parents could also include a time of family prayer, or a reminder to their children that they are also loved by God.

Chapter One

For some teens, pressure from friends and the uncertainty of adolescence can become too much, leading to depression and, in some cases, suicide. In 2011, according to a survey conducted by the Centers for Disease Control and Prevention, 15.8 percent of American high school students had seriously considered suicide in the previous 12 months.

Rock Bottom

Everyone who knew David Hurcombe believed the boy had a bright future ahead. The 17-year-old was going to school to become an electrician. He had plenty of friends, enjoyed parties, and loved music. "He was inquisitive and interested in the meaning of life," said David's friend Michael Carroll. "He was fascinated with computer and electrical projects."

But David had a dark and troubled side as well. One day in October David climbed a concrete wall that separated the platform from the tracks at a commuter train station near his home. When a train emerged from the tunnel, David Hurcombe jumped in front of it and was killed instantly.

The coroner's office conducted an inquest to find out why such a bright young man with a promising future would take his own life. Investigators learned that David had recently been teased by friends about his sexual orientation; David was not gay, but his friends had seen him

Teen Awareness of Suicide

A large percentage of American teens seem to have had at least some personal connection to the subject of suicide.

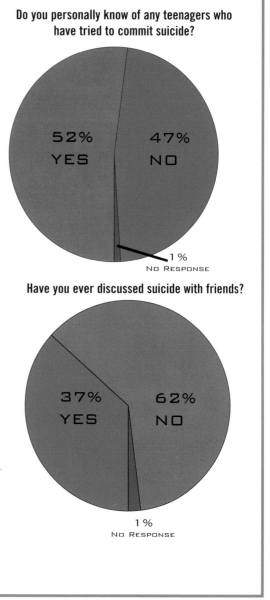

Do you personally know of any teenagers who have tried to commit suicide?

52% YES

47% NO

1% NO RESPONSE

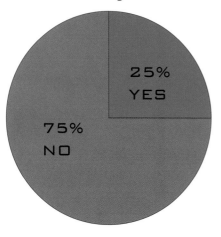

Have you ever talked or thought about committing suicide?

25% YES

75% NO

Have you ever discussed suicide with friends?

37% YES

62% NO

1% NO RESPONSE

Poll taken January–February 2003; 1,200 total respondents.
Source: Gallup Youth Survey/The Gallup Organization

talking with a homosexual man at a party and they tauntingly suggested to David that he was gay as well. Most kids David's age are mature enough to laugh off such teasing, but David was clearly bothered by his friends' insinuations. "David kept asking whether the comment was serious," said Carroll. "He kept referring to whether we all thought he was homosexual. None of our group of friends thought he was one; we told him so but it preyed on his mind."

More answers emerged after investigators had an opportunity to look through David's possessions at home. They found a crumpled suicide note that ended with a dark and haunting joke: "Anyway, got to go, miss my train, see y'all in hell." The note also contained the lyrics to the song "Rock Bottom," written and recorded by Eminem, in which the singer raps about the release of suicide:

> Tired of being hired and fired on the same day . . . you know the rules to the game, play . . . 'Cause when we die we know we're all going the same way . . .

Eminem's lyrics tap into the anxiety and alienation that many teenagers feel. In the United States, 4,600 Americans aged 15 to 24 committed suicide in 2010, according to the Centers for Disease Control and Prevention (CDC). Suicide is the third-leading cause of death among young Americans, behind motor vehicle accidents and homicides.

Adults may find these statistics shocking, but most young people are well aware of the problem. In a 2003 survey of American teenagers conducted by The Gallup Organization, 52 percent of teens between the ages of 13 and 17 who participated in the poll personally know of a friend or family member in their age group who had tried to commit suicide. Furthermore, 37 percent of the teens who responded to the poll said they had discussed suicide with their friends. About 1,200 teenagers participated in the poll, part of the Gallup Organization's long-term project tracking the attitudes and opinions of young people, known as the Gallup Youth Survey.

"The high percentage of teens who report that they have heard suicide discussed may reflect very casual mentions," commented

EMINEM

"Rock Bottom" isn't the only song in which Eminem has raised the topic of teen suicide. In his song "My Name Is" the rapper sings these lyrics:

> Well since age twelve, I've felt like I'm someone else . . . Cause I hung my original self from the top bunk with a belt . . .

The song—Eminem's breakthrough hit—has an intense beat that caught the ear of advertising executives working for the National Football League. They decided to use it in a television commercial promoting NFL games. The commercial aired dozens of times during the 2002 season, until league officials realized the song contained lyrics that addressed adolescent suicide and other controversial topics. NFL officials quickly pulled the ads.

Eminem, whose real name is Marshall Mathers, ascended to rap stardom following a troubled childhood in the working-class neighborhoods of St. Joseph, Missouri, and Detroit, Michigan. While growing up, the singer was very close to his Uncle Ronnie, who was not much more than a teenager himself when he died from a self-inflicted gunshot wound. Young Marshall was said to have been devastated by the suicide of his uncle.

Rick Blizzard, a health care consultant to the Gallup Organization. "But the high percentage of teens who answer positively to these questions about suicide suggests that it is a real issue for teenagers today."

Another troubling revelation in the Gallup Youth Survey's poll was the number of respondents who admitted that they had enter-

By the time he was fourteen, Mathers was already performing under the name M&M, which he later changed to Eminem. He had some recording success in the mid-1990s, but problems with his family and girlfriend led to drug and alcohol abuse. At one point during this period, Eminem hit rock bottom himself. He attempted to commit suicide by taking an overdose of Tylenol, a common non-prescription pain reliever. He later said, "I took a lot of them, I took a bunch of pain killers—Tylenol. I took 13, 16 of 'em and . . . threw 'em up. I thought I was going to die. I thought I was going to die for real."

Eminem emerged from that experience determined to get on with his life. He became a protégé of the rap star Dr Dre, and his music took on a dark and somber tone. Certainly, he captured the attention of American teenagers. In 2000, when the Gallup Youth Survey asked 500 American teenagers to name their heroes, pop music stars placed third at 8 percent (after family members and athletes), with Eminem and Janet Jackson identified as heroes.

Despite his success, Eminem's life remained dark and troubled. He faced criminal charges for assault as well as for illegally possessing a weapon. In 2000 the rapper's wife, Kimberly, attempted suicide. And David Hurcombe was not the only young Eminem fan to have committed suicide. In March 2001, a thirteen-year-old girl named Kaylieh Davies was found dead, the victim of a suicide by hanging. Evidence reported at an inquest by the local coroner indicated that Kaylieh had drawn pictures of hangings in her diary after listening to the rap singer's music. "Some of the CDs I let her listen to, Eminem and Dr Dre, talked about suicide," said Kaylieh's father, Martin Davies. "I guess she had it on her mind."

In 2011, a video for the rapper's song "Space Bound," was criticized by some in the media for its graphic depiction of murder and suicide.

tained notions of committing suicide themselves. Some 25 percent of the respondents answered "yes" to this question, with 7 percent admitting that they had taken at least initial steps toward actually committing the act.

In 2007, according to statistics from the National Institute of Mental Health (NIMH), the suicide rate for Americans ages 15–19 was 6.9 per 100,000. In other words, about one of every 14,500 people in the age group took his or her own life. The suicide rate for children ages 10–14 was 0.9 per 100,000.

Boys are much more likely to commit suicide than girls. For every girl between 15 and 19 years old who takes her own life, nearly five boys in the same age group will take theirs.

"Teen suicide is an emotional cancer at the heart of our 'successful society,' but it has remained, for the most part, a hidden, silent crisis," says Dr. William S. Pollack, assistant clinical professor of psychiatry at Harvard Medical School. "This major dilemma for American families, schools, children, and the entire fabric of our culture has remained almost completely unaddressed or inadequately responded to. This is especially troubling when those of us who have studied, researched, and witnessed this pain I refer to as 'self-murder' know it can be dramatically improved, if not eradicated."

Young people find many reasons to take their own lives. Some of them suffer from mental illness; their symptoms either aren't recognized or are neglected, or the teens receive improper treatment. Other adolescents have substance abuse problems, which can be a contributing factor in suicide cases. In recent years, researchers have found that many young victims have a family history of suicide. Other young people find they can't cope with trouble at home or school. Like David Hurcombe, they may have trouble with their friends.

For many people, the news that a friend or family member has taken his or her own life does not come as a surprise. Adolescent suicide victims often show many warning signs. For others, though, the news comes as a complete shock. That was true in David Hurcombe's case. David's mother, Lynne, said, "He was a happy, sensitive, caring young man who was no trouble at home and who enjoyed life." Yet Hamish Turner, the coroner who investigated David's death, concluded that the boy felt a deep depression because of his friends' remarks about his sexual orientation.

According to the Gallup Youth Survey, many teens feel alienated from society, and admit to feeling confused, pressured, afraid, and angry.

There is no question that teenagers often have difficulty coping with life's challenges. In 1997, the Gallup Youth Survey published a "Teen Alienation Index" and found that about 20 percent of the young people who participated in the poll scored "high" in the index. Such teens admitted to feeling confused, pressured, ignored, bored, lonely, afraid, angry, or tired. These teenagers also admitted to harboring thoughts of doing violence to themselves or others. About 500 teenagers participated in this survey.

Suicide is, of course, a problem that affects more than just teenagers. According to the CDC, suicide was the 10th-leading cause of death among all age groups in 2010. That year, more than 38,000 Americans intentionally killed themselves—a number representing 1.5 percent of all deaths that occurred in the United States.

It's estimated that an American dies by suicide every 14 minutes. Suicides currently outnumber homicides in the United States by more than two to one. In about half of all suicide deaths, the person uses a gun.

When a person commits suicide, family, friends, and even the community can be devastated. Just as awful, though, is what may happen if the suicide attempt fails. Some people recover from their attempts to kill themselves, find the emotional or psychiatric help they need, and carry on with their lives. But what happens to the person who attempts suicide and fails, and is forced to live with the wounds for the rest of his or her life? The damage caused by a failed suicide attempt may be physical as well as emotional. Perhaps this person has become debilitated in some way—brain-damaged, confined to a wheelchair, unable to work or enjoy a full life. A young person who attempts suicide and fails may spend the next 50 or 60 years living with self-inflicted physical wounds.

Estimates vary widely, but as many as 25 unsuccessful suicide attempts may be made for every attempt that is successful. Women and young people frequently fail at their first attempts; adult males, on the other hand, seem to be much better at killing themselves on their first tries. Statistics show that three times as many women as men try suicide but fail.

"After the attempt, one must face the reality of having made such a ghastly choice," says psychologist Richard A. Heckler, who has written extensively on people who survive suicide attempts. "The body suffers from degrees of trauma, and the spirit is left weak and fragile. One can barely conceive of a starting point more tenuous and devoid of promise."

Chapter Two

When a young person talks about suicide—even in what appears to be a casual way—friends should take the person seriously. They should listen carefully, urge their friend to get professional help, and consider sharing their concerns with a trusted adult.

Warning Signs and Risk Factors

The suicide of a young person can do more than traumatize the victim's family and friends. Sometimes a whole community can feel the pain. That's what happened in the small town of Quakertown, Pennsylvania, in the fall of 1983 when two friends, 17-year-old Marc Landis and 16-year-old Dan Ferdock, jumped 200 feet to their deaths into a quarry.

As often occurs in such cases, friends and family members were shocked when they learned of the deaths. No one in the small community, which is located about 40 miles north of Philadelphia, realized the two boys had been troubled.

Soon, evidence was uncovered that suggested the two boys had consumed the drug LSD shortly before their deaths, and that they made a tape recording of the words they uttered during the final few minutes of their lives as they stood on the rocky ledge of the quarry and prepared to jump. After authorities released these sensational details

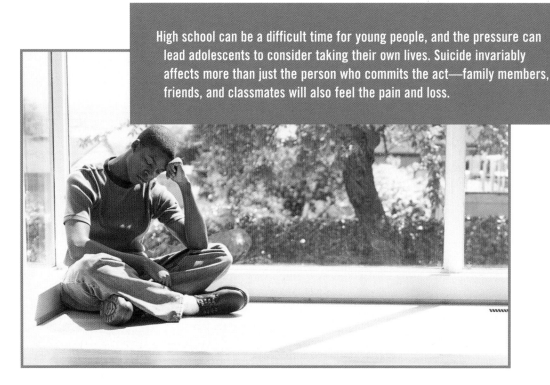

High school can be a difficult time for young people, and the pressure can lead adolescents to consider taking their own lives. Suicide invariably affects more than just the person who commits the act—family members, friends, and classmates will also feel the pain and loss.

of the case, Quakertown found itself invaded by out-of-town reporters and TV news crews. Friends and classmates of Landis and Ferdock, still dealing with their own grief, had to also deal with the attention of the news media. It was a difficult period for everyone at Quakertown High School.

For Michelle Qurashi, the pressure proved to be unbearable. Michelle had been Marc Landis's girlfriend and had been despondent over her boyfriend's death. Two months after the Landis and Ferdock suicides, the 16-year-old Quakertown High School student shot herself in the chest. She died instantly.

In response to the three suicides, many people living in the tiny community went into a fit of despair for months. Media attention grew even more intense. School officials hired psychologists to counsel the students and created a panel of parents and teachers to intervene when young people exhibited signs of self-destruction. "We will not close the doors to this issue and treat it as if nothing has happened," insisted James Beerer, the local high school principal. "It's going to be addressed."

Public health officials have long known that suicides sometimes occur in clusters. In a phenomenon known as "suicide contagion," one person's suicide triggers other vulnerable people to kill themselves—especially adolescents and young adults who have previously thought about or attempted suicide. Surprisingly, perhaps, some research indicates that young people who were close to a previous suicide victim are actually less likely to take their own lives than are strangers to the suicide victim. Some researchers suspect that suicide contagion may be fueled by media coverage, particularly when that coverage is sensationalistic or romanticizes the loss of a young life. However, establishing a precise cause for a suicide cluster is often impossible.

Shortly after the suicide of Quakertown's Michelle Qurashi, people who knew her reported that weeks earlier she had made an unsuccessful attempt to kill herself by taking an overdose of sleeping pills. "I knew she would probably do it," said her friend, Paul Saitta. "I'm going to wonder when it's all going to stop."

The death of Michelle Qurashi was not the only suicide to have occurred in the Quakertown area following the deaths of Landis and Ferdock. In the weeks after the deaths of the two boys, local newspapers reported two other suicides—one involving a 20-year-old woman, the other a 29-year-old woman. Both cases mirrored the incidents involving the three students. In one case, the victim shot herself in the chest; in the other incident, the victim plummeted off a rock-climbers' cliff not far from the quarry where Ferdock and Landis died.

The Warning Signs of Suicide

Following the deaths of Landis and Ferdock, school officials said they feared a "ripple effect" and had taken steps to educate teachers and other staff members on the warning signs of adolescent suicide. Sadly, they missed those signs in Michelle Qurashi.

One of the warning signs that a young person may be contemplating suicide is mood swings. Mood changes may not necessarily be toward sadness, though. People who were formerly quiet may become hyperactive. People who were friendly and outgoing may become withdrawn.

Everyone has times when they feel sad but most people are able to snap out of it and carry on with their lives. Some people, though, have trouble putting depression behind them. Their feelings of sadness linger for a long time. People who are clinically depressed often have trouble getting out of bed. They may not sleep well at night and find themselves waking up early. They may feel the need to take naps during the day.

Depressed people may exhibit changes in their appetites. They may have lost a lot of weight in a short period of time or they may have gained a lot of weight quickly. Depressed people may feel restless or uncomfortable around friends and family members.

They may find it difficult to concentrate or they may lose interest in hobbies or other activities they once enjoyed. They may start giving away their possessions, as though they are preparing for death. Older people who prepare for suicide may make out a will, although this would be unusual behavior for an adolescent.

Potential suicide victims may make a half-hearted attempt to kill themselves using a method they think won't work. That may have happened in Michelle Qurashi's first suicide attempt. Or they may start taking risks with their lives, such as driving recklessly.

Potential suicide victims may start drinking or taking drugs. They may lose interest in their personal appearance. They may become pre-occupied with death. Mostly, they find themselves entertaining thoughts that life is not worth living.

Research indicates that young people are often quite verbal with their intentions. They may make statements such as "I'd be better off dead" or "I won't be a problem for you much longer" or "Nothing matters; it's no use."

Although suicide victims may show warning signs, experts agree that there is no definitive way to predict suicidal behavior. After all, just because a young person starts acting depressed or impulsively doesn't mean that person intends to take his or her own life. And although researchers have identified factors that place individuals at higher risk for suicide, very few young people with these risk factors will actually commit suicide. Suicide is a relatively rare event and it is therefore difficult to predict which young people who exhibit these risk factors will ultimately commit suicide.

Dr. Jan Fawcett, chairperson of the Psychiatry Department at Rush-Presbyterian St. Luke's Medical Center in Chicago, says that the people who can best identify youths at risk are mental health professionals, but statistics show that more than half of all individuals who commit suicide had no recent contact with psychiatrists or psychologists who might have helped prevent the suicide by making sure the troubled teenagers received help.

Fawcett says improving access to treatment is critical to preventing the suicides in young people. "The standard behaviors used to identify persons at risk fall seriously short of the task of identifying individuals in the days and weeks leading up to their suicidal behavior," notes Fawcett. Another sad fact, though, is that young people still do commit suicide even if they are receiving treatment.

Who Is at Risk?

Suicide among young people is a significant problem. However, it is the elderly—particularly older white males—who are most likely to commit suicide. Among white males 65 and older, risk goes up with age. White men 85 and older have a suicide rate that is six times that of the overall national rate. Some older persons may not survive attempts to kill themselves because they are less likely to recuperate from the damage they do to their bodies. More than 70 percent of older suicide victims have visited their physicians within the month that preceded their deaths. Many of those elderly suicide victims did not tell their doctors they were depressed, nor did the doctor detect it. This has led to efforts by researchers to determine how to best improve physicians' abilities to detect and treat depression in older adults.

Statistics show that any young person can fall victim to suicide. Straight-A students and gifted student athletes have taken their own lives. So have students who struggle in school, seem to have no interest in athletics or other extracurricular activities, and find themselves at odds with the law. Students who simply seem to blend into the crowd are also at risk.

Those young people would seem to have little in common with one another, but as investigators piece together the stories of their lives, they find that there are many things that are common among suicide victims.

Teenagers experience strong feelings of stress, confusion, self-doubt, pressure to succeed, financial uncertainty and other fears while growing up. Some teenagers may find the break-up of their parents' marriage too traumatic an experience to face. Or, perhaps they harbor deep feelings of stress over the remarriage of their parents and the formation of new families in which they are forced to share a home with stepparents or new siblings. Perhaps the divorce and remarriage has forced them to move to a new community and enroll in a new school where they have no friends. Suicide offers a solution to these seemingly insurmountable problems.

Among American college students, suicide ranks behind only motor vehicle accidents as the leading cause of death. A recent NIMH estimate placed the annual number of collegiate suicides at about 1,100. In a survey conducted in spring 2012 by the American College Health Association, 4.9 percent of the more than 25,000 respondents said they had seriously considered suicide in the previous 12 months. Nearly one of every hundred

The rate of suicide among older people is even greater than the rate among young adults. The suicide rate of white men older than 85 is six times higher than the national average.

respondents (0.8 percent) admitted to attempting suicide in the previous 12 months.

Some aspects of college life may increase the risk of suicide, at least for certain young people. (However, it must be pointed out that a large 2011 study, "Leading Causes of Mortality Among American College Students," found that the suicide rate for college students was considerably lower than the rate for the age group as a whole.) Many college students find themselves away from home for the first time. They are confronted with an unfamiliar environment and new people, and they don't have their parents and other familiar faces nearby to support them

ASSISTED SUICIDE

One issue that rarely involves young people is assisted suicide—the practice whereby a person who wants to commit suicide is aided by another person (often a physician who provides a fatal dose of medication). Assisted suicide is illegal in most countries. As of 2013, it was legal—under certain fairly narrow circumstances—in the United States only in Montana, Oregon, and Washington. The issue of assisted suicide rose to prominence in the 1980s and 1990s mostly through the activities of Dr. Jack Kevorkian, a Michigan physician who helped many people end their own lives. In the media, he became known as "Dr. Death."

In all cases, Dr. Kevorkian's patients were older adults who suffered through years of painful illnesses such as cancer. Kevorkian and others insisted they should have the "right to die" and that suicide could be a rational decision. Others have argued that suicide is never a rational decision and that it is the result of depression, anxiety, and fear of being dependent or a burden.

Surveys of terminally ill people indicate that very few of them consider taking their own lives, and when they do it is often in the context of depression. Studies also suggest that assisted suicide is more acceptable by the public and health providers for the old who are ill or disabled, compared to young people who are ill or disabled.

during difficult times. They may not get enough sleep, either because of their study habits or because of the typical college social scene. They may not eat right. Add in the pressures of meeting the academic requirements of college, and it is easy to see why many students have difficulty coping.

"The nature of the campus environment itself may serve to exacerbate any existing symptoms or engender the expression of emotional or behavioral disorders in those students who may be predisposed to mental illness," the National Mental Health

For 10 years, Dr. Kevorkian was able to help people commit suicide by providing them with drugs they could administer to themselves. He was arrested and charged with criminal offenses four times, but always beat the charges, winning acquittals from sympathetic juries. In 1998, though, he crossed the line when he actually gave a man a lethal injection of drugs. He also taped the act and submitted it to TV networks for broadcast, essentially daring prosecutors to charge him with murder. "When society reaches the age of enlightenment, then they'll call me and other doctors 'Dr. Life,'" Kevorkian said.

He was arrested, charged with murder, and convicted. In 1999, Kevorkian was sentenced to 10 to 25 years in prison. He was released in 2007 and died four years later.

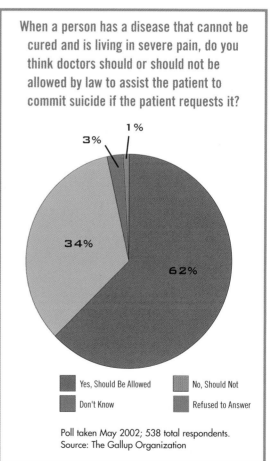

When a person has a disease that cannot be cured and is living in severe pain, do you think doctors should or should not be allowed by law to assist the patient to commit suicide if the patient requests it?

1%
3%
34%
62%

■ Yes, Should Be Allowed   ■ No, Should Not
■ Don't Know   ■ Refused to Answer

Poll taken May 2002; 538 total respondents.
Source: The Gallup Organization

Association (now called Mental Health America) said in a report published in 2002.

And yet, there are far more reasons for the high suicide rate on college campuses. The report suggested that colleges themselves might be partly at fault for not providing students with adequate psychiatric counseling. "There may be a group of students who are not being diagnosed and who may be overlooked when it comes to receiving adequate treatment and supportive services," the organization said.

The report recommended that colleges examine the mental health services they offer to students. Among the suggestions included in the report were screening programs to identify students at risk; educational programs for faculty members, coaches, and other college staff members to help them identify students at risk; establishment of on-site campus counseling centers; stress reduction programs for students; a support network made up of students; assistance from off-campus mental health professionals; a reliable system of emergency medical assistance; follow-up programs to keep track of the progress of students who have been identified as suicide risks; and policies that enable students to take leaves from their classes when necessary.

Additional Risk Factors

There is growing evidence that indicates a family history of suicide can contribute to the likelihood that a young person will try to take his or her life. A high-profile example of this was rock star Kurt Cobain, who killed himself in 1994. Cobain was the third member of his family to take his own life.

Medical researchers are just starting to look at genetic factors as a contributor to the risk for suicidal behavior. Major psychiatric illnesses, including bipolar disorder, depression, schizophrenia, alcoholism and drug abuse, and certain personality disorders which run in families, increase the risk for suicidal behavior. This does not mean that suicidal behavior is inevitable for young people with a family history of suicide; it simply means that such people may be more vulnerable and should take steps to reduce their risk, such as getting evaluation and treatment at the first sign of mental illness.

A number of recent national surveys have helped shed light on the relationship between alcohol and drug use and suicidal behavior. A review of suicides among young people between the ages of 18 and 20 found that drinking was associated with high-

For some teens the stress caused by family problems may become too much to handle. Current statistics indicate that 40 to 50 percent of marriages in the United States will end in divorce.

er youth suicide rates in states that were among the last to raise their minimum drinking ages to 21.

In studies that examine risk factors among people who have completed suicide, drug and alcohol abuse occurs more frequently among young people compared to older persons. Alcohol and substance abuse problems contribute to suicidal behavior in several ways. Persons who are dependent on substances often have a number of other risk factors for suicide. In addition to being depressed, they are also likely to have social and financial problems. Substance abuse can be common among young people who are prone to be impulsive, and among teenagers who engage in many types of high-risk behaviors. In other words, those teenagers who are driving recklessly may also be drinking before they get behind the wheel of a car.

Teenagers sometimes act with little regard to what would truly be the most responsible thing to do. But impulsive behavior is part of being a teenager. Most young people stop acting on impulse as they mature.

Nevertheless, research clearly indicates that suicide victims often act impulsively. Psychiatrists believe impulsive behavior that rises to the level of destructive behavior could also be a symptom of a number of mental disorders. They have linked impulsiveness with personality disorders among young females. Boys who drink or abuse drugs also exhibit signs of impulsive behavior.

Teenage boys who act up or are otherwise antisocial often suffer from impulsiveness. Indeed, impulsive behavior among boys has been linked with aggressive and violent behavior that occasionally results not only in suicidal tendencies, but homicidal acts as well. However, impulsiveness among boys doesn't always manifest itself in aggressive behavior. Impulsive boys who are very well behaved may be suicide victims as well.

* * *

If you are aware of a friend talking about suicide, you should take their distress seriously, listen to what they have to say and help them get to a professional for evaluation and treatment. People consider suicide when they are hopeless and unable to see alternative solutions to problems. If you believe a friend or family member is in imminent danger of harming himself or herself, do not leave the person alone. You may need to take emergency steps to get help, such as calling 911.

Chapter Three

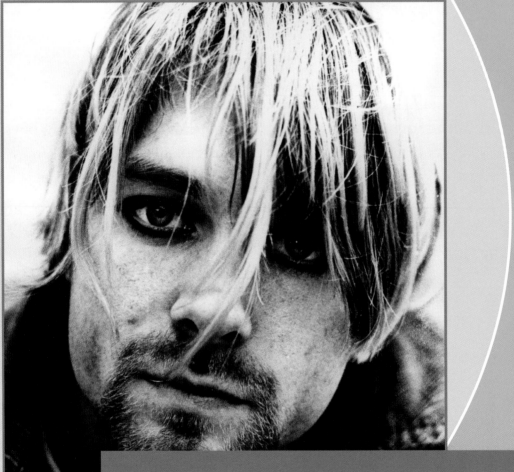

As a youth, Kurt Cobain told his friends, "I am going to be a superstar musician, kill myself and go out in a flame of glory." This prediction sadly came true. The influential lead singer of the grunge band Nirvana was called the "poet of pain" for his powerful lyrics about teenage feelings of alienation and angst. He committed suicide on April 5, 1994.

Mental Illness and Suicide

No one who knew Kurt Cobain was surprised when the founder and lead singer of the grunge rock band Nirvana took his own life in 1994. The musician had struggled with mental illness for most of his life. In addition, he had a substance abuse problem, a family history of suicide, hostility toward the fame he found as a rock star, and a preoccupation with death.

Cobain was no teenager when he took his own life; he was a 27-year-old husband and father. Still, he was not a maturing adult with a stable home life. "I am on the educated level of about 10th grade in high school," he wrote shortly before his death.

During the final few years of his life Cobain kept copious journals, constantly writing down his ideas and impressions of life. They were hardly diaries; mostly, he just let his thoughts run on, using his pen to record a confusing and depressed ramble that often came back to one common topic:

his own death. On one occasion, he wrote, "I was actually enjoying doing rebellious things like stealing this booze and busting store windows, getting in fistfights, etc. . . . and nothing ever mattered. I decided within the next month I'll not sit on my roof and think about jumping but I'll actually kill myself." Another entry reads, "This little pit-stop we call life, that we so seriously worry about, is nothing but a small, over-the-weekend jail sentence, compared to what will come with death." Yet the same pen that authored such troubling words also wrote Nirvana's biggest hits.

Kurt Cobain had been born into a broken home in a working-class community near Seattle, Washington, on February 20, 1967. In the late 1980s and early 1990s, he and his band mates helped launch the era of grunge rock. They wore scruffy bluejeans and flannel shirts, and their music was as gritty as their clothes. Nirvana's music captured the flavor of teenage angst and alienation, and no song voiced these feelings better than the band's first hit, "Smells Like Teen Spirit." Teenagers everywhere heard their message and responded. On January 11, 1992, Nirvana's album *Nevermind* reached the top spot on *Billboard* magazine's chart of best-selling albums.

Cobain's lyrics appealed to the so-called "Generation X"—a generation of young people who did not hold out much hope for the future. In 1993, when Nirvana was at the height of its popularity, a Gallup Youth Survey found teenagers admitting to some risky behavior. That year, the Gallup Organization polled young people between the ages of 13 and 17. The organization found that 20 percent of the boys and 19 percent of the girls "did something that is risky just for kicks." In addition, 7 percent of the boys and 15 percent of the girls "felt life was not worth living." Clearly, Kurt Cobain had his thumb on the pulse of American youth.

"Cobain's music and lyrics confronted and changed me," wrote Jamie Allen, an Atlanta-based writer who wrote an essay on the singer for Salon.com. "They forced me to see a world I had previously avoided, mainly because my friends and I never walked that direction. Cobain was the first writer from my own age group to capture my attention."

However, it should not have been surprising that the artist who gave voice to that generation was himself besieged by confusing and contradictory thoughts and internal demons so angry that

The members of Nirvana are shown at a music awards ceremony. Kurt Cobain (third from left) appears to be under the influence of drugs. He suffered from a stomach condition, and found that opiates such as heroin were the only things that dulled the pain. Both Cobain's mental illness and his drug abuse probably contributed to his decision to end his life.

during the final few years of his life he had just a vague notion of where reality ended and insanity began.

Kurt Cobain's death was typical in that most suicide victims believe they have become a burden on others. Like many suicide victims, Cobain left a note. It was addressed to his wife, the singer Courtney Love, and their daughter Frances. The note said Cobain had lost his love for music and performing. "I feel guilty beyond words for these things," he said. And then he ended his note, putting down in black and white the way he had always envisioned his life to end. "Thank you from the pit of my burning nauseous stomach for your letters and concern during the last year," he wrote. "I'm too much of a neurotic moody person and I don't have the passion anymore, so remember, it's better to burn out, than to fade away. Peace, love, empathy, Kurt Cobain."

Suicide and Bipolar Disorder

Kurt Cobain suffered from what is clinically known as bipolar disorder. This condition—also known as manic depression—is characterized by episodes of abnormally elevated mood (mania), which typically alternate with episodes of deep depression. It is believed that more than 2 million people in America suffer from bipolar disorder. Typically, the disease first manifests itself in adolescents. There is no known cure, although bipolar disorder can be treated with counseling and medication.

During manic periods, people with bipolar disorder have a high level of energy. They can be impulsive and reckless. Their speech can be rapid. They may feel empowered by their outlandish ideas and activities. They may feel euphoric—on top of the world—and no amount of bad news can change that. On the other hand, during manic periods people with bipolar disorder are also prone to extreme irritability during manic episodes. They may snap out at a friend if their ideas or plans are challenged. Often they don't feel the need to sleep, but may gulp down sleeping pills to help them rest. They may be overconfident in their abilities and take on projects or jobs that are too ambitious. They exhibit poor judgment, which may lead to irrational behavior, such as reckless driving or spending sprees. Heavy drinking and use of drugs is also common.

During depressive episodes, people with bipolar disorder experience extreme sadness or hopelessness. They lack energy and may find it difficult or impossible just to get out of bed.

Many people with bipolar disorder complain of physical ills, such as headaches and stomach aches. That was particularly true in Cobain's case. His journal entries and even his suicide note contain references to a chronically upset stomach. And, of course, many people with bipolar disorder dwell on death, suicide, and other forms of self-destructive behavior.

"Kurt was diagnosed at a young age with Attention Deficit Disorder, then later with bipolar disorder," said his cousin, Beverly Cobain, a nurse and author. "Bipolar disorder has the same characteristics as major clinical depression, but with mood swings, which present as rage, euphoria, high energy, irritability, distractibility, overconfidence, and other symptoms. As Kurt undoubtedly knew, bipolar illness can be very difficult to manage, and the correct diagnosis is critical. Unfortunately for Kurt, compliance with the appropriate treatment is also a critical factor."

Certainly, Kurt Cobain's other problems, most notably his heroin and alcohol habits, were contributing factors, but there is no question that bipolar disorder added to his risk of suicide. "His risk was very high," observed Beverly Cobain. "Untreated bipolar disorder, drug addiction, prior suicides of family members, alcohol, violence and unpredictability in his childhood, [low] self-esteem, violence in his married life. Kurt could have been a poster child for the risk of suicide."

There is no scientific proof that bipolar disorder is inherited, but according to Mental Health America at least 80 percent of patients diagnosed with bipolar disorder have relatives who also suffer from some form of depression. Researchers believe that the violent mood swings typical in victims of bipolar disorder may be caused by a chemical imbalance in the body. This imbalance may be attributed to a lack of certain hormones—the chemicals in peo-

SYMPTOMS OF BIPOLAR DISORDER

Bipolar disorder causes dramatic mood swings—from highs (mania) to lows (depression). Great changes in energy and behavior often accompany these mood changes.

Signs and symptoms of mania (or a manic episode) include:

- Increased energy, activity, and restlessness
- Excessively "high," overly good, euphoric mood
- Extreme irritability
- Racing thoughts; jumping from one idea to another
- Distractibility; inability to concentrate
- Little sleep needed
- Unrealistic beliefs in one's abilities and powers
- Poor judgment
- A lasting period of behavior that is different from usual
- Abuse of drugs
- Provocative, intrusive, or aggressive behavior
- Denial that anything is wrong

A manic episode is diagnosed if elevated mood occurs with three or more of the other symptoms most of the day, nearly every day, for one week or longer. If the mood is irritable, four additional symptoms must be present.

ple's bodies that regulate how they grow, how healthy they are, how well they reproduce, and how well their organs function.

In recent years, medical researchers have started studying the chemicals in the brain known as neurotransmitters to determine whether they can be the cause of bipolar disorder. These neurotransmitters act as messengers, delivering information to nerve cells. It has been determined that depressed people and suicide victims lack a sufficient amount of the tiny pump-like components that deliver the neurotransmitter known as serotonin to the brain. Therefore, the serotonin is delivered to the brain in unregulated quantities, which could account for the violent mood swings asso-

Signs and symptoms of depression (or a depressive episode) include:

- Lasting sad, anxious, or empty mood
- Feelings of hopelessness or pessimism
- Feelings of guilt, worthlessness, or helplessness
- Loss of interest or pleasure in activities once enjoyed
- Decreased energy, a feeling of fatigue or of being "slowed down"
- Difficulty concentrating, remembering, or making decisions
- Restlessness or irritability
- Sleeping too much, or inability to sleep
- Chronic pain or other persistent bodily symptoms that are not caused by physical illness or injury
- Thoughts of death or suicide, or suicide attempts

A depressive episode is diagnosed if five or more of these symptoms last most of the day, nearly every day, for a period of two weeks or longer.

Source: National Institutes of Mental Health

Bipolar disorder, also known as manic-depression, is a brain disorder that causes unusual shifts in a person's mood, energy, and ability to function. A person can swing from a euphoric, high-energy state to deep feelings of depression within a very short time.

ciated with bipolar disorder. "Clearly, there is overlap between the disorders because major depression is a significant risk factor for suicide," says a report by the National Institute of Mental Health.

There is no cure for manic depression. Bipolar disorder is treated with medication, counseling, and support from family members. Some of the medications are designed to regulate or increase serotonin levels.

Bipolar disorder is characterized by an extreme degree of depression. A lesser degree is known as "dysthymia." In dysthymia, the symptoms are similar to other forms of depression but they are not as pronounced. People who suffer from dysthymic disorder may experience long-term and chronic feelings of physical illness or a lack of interest in activities they formerly found enjoyable. The symptoms can be episodic, meaning they come and go. Psychiatrists look for the symptoms to last at least two years before they render a diagnosis of dysthymia. In most cases, patients start exhibiting symptoms of dysthymia in their late teenage years. The onset of the symptoms is gradual; they can take years to manifest themselves.

Unlike others who suffer from depression, the prognosis for dysthymics is often good. According to the World Health Organization, half the sufferers of dysthymia do recover and go on to lead normal lives.

Although dysthymic patients do not display all of the symptoms of a manic-depressive, that does not mean they aren't at risk to commit suicide. A study conducted in 1988 of adolescent suicide victims in the Pittsburgh area found a significant number of them had been diagnosed with dysthymia.

Experts estimate that more than 90 percent of the people who commit suicide suffer from depression and other mental disorders, or have a substance-abuse problem (often in combination with depression). However, only a small minority of people who suffer from depression (2 to 9 percent, according to researchers at the Mayo Clinic) will commit suicide. In fact, many people overcome depression and live fulfilling and pro-

ductive lives, especially if they receive treatment from mental health professionals.

"Depression is not the same as suicide," reported the *Journal of Nervous and Mental Disease* in 1993. "For one thing, they have enormously different fatality rates. One can live a long, unhappy life with depression, but many people—too many—have died of suicide. Suicide is not a psychiatric disorder. All persons who commit suicide—100 percent of them—are perturbed, but they are not necessarily clinically depressed or schizophrenic or alcoholic or addicted or psychiatrically ill."

Suicide and Eating Disorders

Another mental illness that has recently been studied as a link to suicide is bulimia nervosa, an eating disorder that primarily afflicts adolescent girls and other young women. Patients who suffer from bulimia nervosa stuff themselves with food (this is called binge eating, or binging) then force themselves to vomit or use laxatives (this is known as purging). Girls who suffer from bulimia nervosa have a morbid fear of getting fat. It is similar to the eating disorder known as anorexia nervosa, in which girls starve themselves.

A 1998 poll by the Gallup Youth Survey found that 92 percent of the 500 teenagers who were questioned said they worried about their weight. That poll also found that 14 percent of the teenagers said they were "disgusted" by overweight people—certainly, one of the emotional building blocks that must be in place for a young person to fall victim to anorexia or bulimia. Another poll of 500 teenagers by the Gallup Organization in 1998 found that 23 percent of the respondents weighed more than they would like. What's more, 31 percent of the teenagers who participated said they had tried to lose weight by going without food, while 8 percent had tried to lose weight by purging.

Medical researchers believe there are many similarities among people who exhibit symptoms of bulimia nervosa and people who talk about suicide or try to kill themselves. Bulimia nervosa is an addictive behavior, much like drug or alcohol abuse. Many bulimics tell their doctors that they find the cycles of binge eating and purging to be a way in which they can relieve anxiety, similar to the way some people seek release from cares through drugs.

Many people who have survived their suicide attempts have reported feeling better about themselves, as though the attempt to do physical harm to themselves helped them find a release from their tensions and anxieties.

And, finally, many bulimics are also diagnosed with depression and are treated with anti-depressant drugs, which is a common treatment for depressed people who attempt suicide.

Chapter Four

A Denver fireman visits a memorial for the victims of the Columbine High School tragedy. The shootings at the school in April 1999 shocked the entire nation. Twelve students and a teacher were killed by two angry students, who then committed suicide.

A Very Different Phenomenon

For the students and teachers at Columbine High School in Littleton, Colorado, April 20, 1999, started as a typical day. Tests were taken, science labs conducted, literature and history and current events discussed. The school chorus rehearsed for an afternoon concert. Students with free periods drifted outside to enjoy a gorgeous spring day.

Two Columbine High School seniors, 18-year-old Eric Harris and 17-year-old Dylan Klebold, were determined that April 20, 1999, would be anything but a typical day for Columbine—or the entire United States, for that matter. Harris and Klebold were planning to die. But before that happened, they wanted to kill as many people as possible.

Suicide is typically a solitary act carried out in private: approximately three-quarters of all suicides, according to the Harvard School of Public Health, take place at the victim's home. On rare occasions, however, a suicidal person (almost

Columbine killers Dylan Klebold (left) and Eric Harris. A panel of leading forensic psychiatrists and psychologists who examined the case for the FBI concluded that Klebold suffered from depression, whereas Harris was a psychopath.

always a male) goes on a murderous rampage as a prelude to killing himself—or forcing the police to kill him, which is commonly referred to as "suicide by cop."

Rampage killers are usually motivated by intense anger stemming from a belief that other people have wronged them. Much of the early news coverage from Columbine explained the actions of Eric Harris and Dylan Klebold as revenge for bullying the two had endured. The reality, however, was much more complicated. Harris, according to a team of prominent psychiatrists and psychologists assembled by the FBI, was a psychopath. In layperson's terms, he lacked a conscience. He considered himself superior to other people, and staging a massacre would demonstrate that superiority. Klebold, by contrast, was angry but also chronically depressed. He frequently contemplated killing himself. Harris apparently enlisted his suicidal friend in the murderous plan he, Harris, had conceived.

That plan called for the detonation of two large propane bombs in the school cafeteria during the first lunch period. As survivors fled the building, Harris and Klebold would gun them down. Harris carried a shotgun and a carbine; Klebold, a shotgun and a semiautomatic handgun.

Around 11:20 A.M., after the propane bombs failed to detonate, Harris and Klebold began shooting students outside the school. Then they entered the building and continued the rampage.

While police arrived on the scene within minutes, they didn't attempt to enter the building until about 12:05 P.M. By that time, Klebold and Harris had killed or fatally wounded 12 students and a teacher. Twenty-one others were wounded but would survive. At 12:08, the killers turned their guns on themselves.

Incidents of mass homicide–suicide, while they understand-ably garner lots of headlines, are rare. Rarer still are incidents of mass homicide–suicide perpetrated by teens and young adults. Yet the toll of such rampages cannot be ignored. In recent years, a handful of troubled young Americans have followed in the foot-steps of Eric Harris and Dylan Klebold, with horrifying results.

Sixteen-year-old Jeffrey Weise went on a shooting spree on March 21, 2005. Weise killed his grandfather and his grandfather's companion. Then, armed with two handguns and a shotgun, he drove to his school, Red Lake Senior High, in Red Lake, Minnesota. There he killed seven people before committing suicide.

Seung-Hui Cho, a 23-year-old student at Virginia Tech, was responsible for a bloodbath on the college's campus in Blacksburg, Virginia. Using two semiautomatic pistols, Cho slaughtered 32 students and teachers, wounding more than 20 others, before killing himself. Cho's rampage took place on April 16, 2007.

On December 5 of the same year, 19-year-old Robert Hawkins entered a shopping mall in Omaha, Nebraska, and opened fire with a semiautomatic rifle. He killed eight people and wounded four before turning the gun on himself.

On the morning of December 14, 2012, Adam Lanza shot and killed his mother inside their home in Newtown, Connecticut. Then the 20-year-old drove to nearby Sandy Hook Elementary School, which he had attended years before. There he killed 20 first-graders and six adult staff members with a military-style semiautomatic rifle. As police arrived at the school, Lanza shot himself in the head with one of the two handguns he was carrying.

The circumstances of these young killers' lives, and their mental states, varied. Weise, diagnosed with depression, had previously attempted suicide and was being treated with Prozac, an antidepressant medication. Some research has linked antidepressant use in children and adolescents to an increased risk of violent and suicidal behavior. Hawkins—who had a history of depression and substance abuse but wasn't under the care of a doctor, had recently broken up with his girlfriend and been fired from his job at a McDonald's restaurant. In a suicide note, he said he would no longer be a burden to his family and would now be famous. Both Cho and Lanza had conditions that made them anxious or uncomfortable in social situations, and neither seems to have had any friends. Cho compared himself to Eric Harris and Dylan Klebold in a bizarre videotape he sent to NBC News before his rampage. Lanza, according to news accounts, was inspired by Norwegian mass shooter Anders Breivik and wanted to "beat" Breivik's body count. In a 2011 spree, Breivik had killed 77 people.

Ready Access to Firearms

While all of the aforementioned killers displayed signs of mental or emotional troubles, that doesn't necessarily mean their rampages could have been anticipated. "People exhibit different kinds of behavior or thinking patterns that could possibly lead to a violent act," forensic psychiatrist Douglas Mossman explains. "But the problem is that there are hundreds of individuals who display these same patterns, who don't go on to act violent."

Nor, even after the fact, is it entirely clear why Weise, Hawkins, Cho, and Lanza went berserk. What is clear, however, is how they carried out their massacres: Each got his hands on at least one

Memorial to the young students murdered at the Sandy Hook Elementary School in Newtown, Connecticut, in December 2012. The shooter, Adam Lanza, committed suicide at the end of his murder spree. Lanza is believed to have suffered from a mental disorder.

firearm capable of firing a large number of rounds rapidly. Cho, for example, fired more than 170 bullets in about 11 minutes with his two semiautomatic pistols. Lanza fired 154 rounds from his assault-style rifle in less than five minutes. All of these massacres reignited a debate that had flared after Columbine: Should the law do more to limit access to guns?

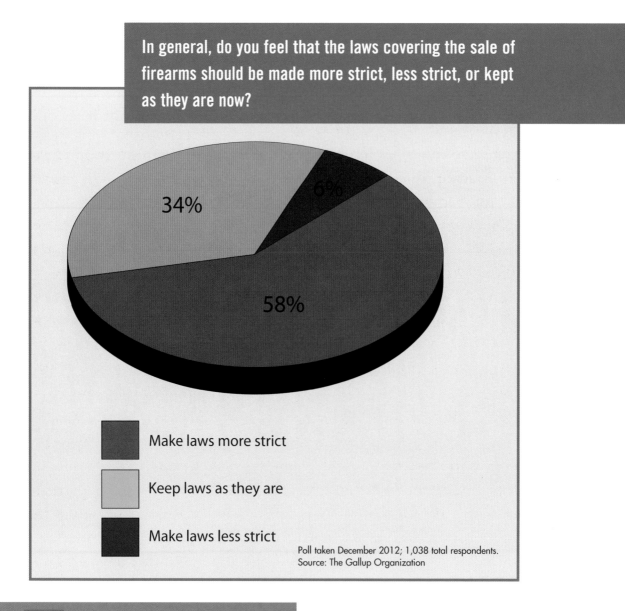

In general, do you feel that the laws covering the sale of firearms should be made more strict, less strict, or kept as they are now?

34%

6%

58%

■ Make laws more strict

■ Keep laws as they are

■ Make laws less strict

Poll taken December 2012; 1,038 total respondents.
Source: The Gallup Organization

In the United States, the purchase and ownership of firearms is regulated—quite loosely and ineffectually, according to critics—by a patchwork of state and federal laws. At the state level, restrictions on who can buy or possess a gun vary widely. As of early 2013, a total of 30 states had no minimum age for the legal possession of a long gun (a rifle or shotgun); in most of the remaining 20 states, as well as the District of Columbia, the minimum age was 18, though 14-year-olds in Montana, and 16-year-olds in New York, could legally own a long gun. In 22 states there was no age requirement for the purchase of handguns. Yet a majority of these states, incongruously, did have age requirements (usually 18 or 21) for the actual possession of handguns.

Federal law, which supersedes state laws, does include minimum-age provisions for the purchase of firearms (18 for long guns; 21 for handguns). However, there is a huge loophole: the provisions apply only to sales by licensed gun dealers. At gun shows or online, unlicensed private sellers may legally sell guns to persons above the minimum age (if any) set by the state where the sale occurs.

That same loophole affected other major provisions of the federal Brady law, which was enacted in 1993. The law was named for James Brady, the presidential press secretary who was shot in the head by a mentally ill assassin who attempted to kill President Ronald Reagan in 1981. Under the Brady law, persons seeking to buy a firearm from a licensed dealer must first fill out an application and undergo a background check through the National Instant Criminal Background Check System (NICS). NICS, which is maintained by the FBI, rejects gun-purchase applications of people who are forbidden under federal law to buy firearms. This includes anyone with a felony record; anyone who has been convicted of a domestic-violence offense, even if it was a misdemeanor; anyone who is subject to a restraining order; anyone who has been committed to a mental institution or who has been judged mentally ill by a court; and anyone who is addicted to drugs. However, the Brady law didn't require unlicensed private sellers to submit gun-purchase applications to NICS. Thus, at gun shows or through online transactions, people legally prohibited from buying a firearm could simply lie about their criminal record or history of mental illness. Weaknesses in the system, gun-control advocates say, have repeatedly been borne out by cases such as Columbine.

Of the four firearms Eric Harris and Dylan Klebold used in the Columbine massacre, they obtained three—two shotguns and a carbine—legally. Yet at the time they got the guns, in late 1998, neither boy was 18—the minimum age for buying a long gun in Colorado. Nor is it clear that either boy would have passed a background check. They were both in a juvenile offender program, the result of their arrests earlier in the year for breaking into a van and stealing electronics equipment. But the boys convinced Robyn Anderson, an 18-year-old friend of Klebold's, to accompany them to a gun show, where she bought the three long guns from private sellers. No law was broken when Anderson gave the guns to Harris and Klebold, as Colorado had no minimum age for the possession of rifles or shotguns.

The fourth gun used in the Columbine shootings was a TEC-9, a highly lethal semiautomatic 9mm pistol. The TEC-9 was obtained illegally, as Colorado law prohibited the provision of handguns to anyone under 18 years of age. Four months before the massacre, Klebold and Harris purchased the gun for $500 illegally from Mark Manes, a systems administrator. Manes and Philip Duran, who worked with Klebold and Harris at a pizza parlor and introduced the boys to Manes, were charged by police with providing a handgun to minors. They each received prison terms—Manes was sentenced to six years in prison, while Duran received a prison sentence of more than four years.

During Duran's sentencing hearing, prosecutors played a videotape they found during the investigation of the murders. The tape had been made by Harris and Klebold about a month before they took their guns to Columbine. In the videotape, the two killers thank Manes and Duran for their help in obtaining the TEC-9. "I'd like to make a thank you to Mark and Phil," Klebold said on the tape. "Very cool. You helped us do what we needed to do." Harris and Klebold were quick to add, though, that if Manes and Duran had not helped them procure the weapon, they would have found someone else who would.

Despite the shocking carnage at Columbine, the massacre didn't lead to

More Americans commit suicide with a gun than through all other methods combined. Among young adults, it is estimated that 60 percent of suicides involve firearms.

changes in gun control laws, either at the state or the federal level. The impetus for change, which seemed strong in the immediate aftermath of Harris and Klebold's rampage, ultimately petered out as the country's focus turned to other issues. That same pattern was repeated after other gun massacres in the years following Columbine. In part, the failure of legislators to address the issue of gun violence reflected the political influence of the National Rifle Association. The NRA, a powerful gun lobby, had a reputation for helping defeat lawmakers who advocated any limitations on access to firearms.

However, there were signs this situation might be changing after the December 2012 massacre at Sandy Hook Elementary School in Newtown, Connecticut. Opinion polls conducted in early 2013 found that huge majorities of Americans supported stricter gun control measures. In Connecticut, Colorado, and Maryland, legislation was passed banning assault weapons, restricting the size of ammunition magazines, and expanding background checks. The U.S. Congress, meanwhile, took up the issue of gun control, though as of spring 2013 it was unclear what, if any, new laws would be enacted.

Guns and Teen Suicide

There is no question that firearms are the primary method of committing suicide, particularly among adolescents. In 2012 the Centers for Disease Control and Prevention reported that nationally, firearms were involved in 45 percent of all suicides committed by people younger than age 24. Teenage boys are more prone to use guns than girls, who frequently try to commit suicide by overdosing on drugs.

Oregon is one of the few states that keeps records on the methods people use to end their own lives. In a study of suicide attempts conducted between 1988 and 1993, researchers in Oregon found that nearly 64 percent of all suicides were performed with guns, while 10 percent were undertaken through drug overdoses. Other methods included poisoning with substances other than drugs, suffocating or hanging, drowning, using knives or other sharp objects, and jumping from high places.

Oregon also keeps statistics on suicide attempts that fail. Not surprisingly, the state determined that a person who uses a gun in a suicide attempt is usually successful. This is particularly true for

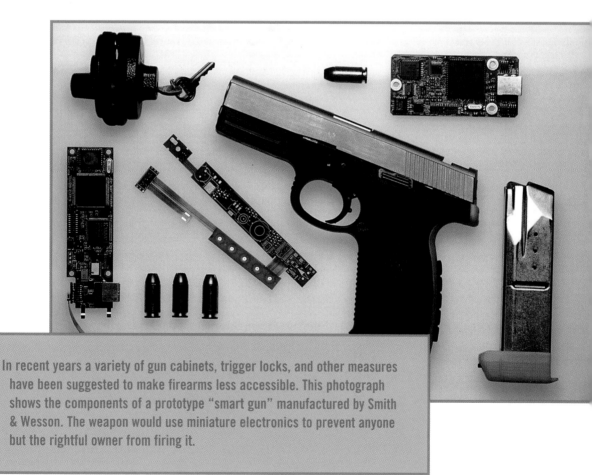

In recent years a variety of gun cabinets, trigger locks, and other measures have been suggested to make firearms less accessible. This photograph shows the components of a prototype "smart gun" manufactured by Smith & Wesson. The weapon would use miniature electronics to prevent anyone but the rightful owner from firing it.

young people. The state found that for teenagers between the ages of 15 and 17, fewer than 1 percent survived a suicide attempt made with a gun. The survival rate for teenagers in that age group who tried drug overdoses was much higher. Oregon researchers found that nearly 75 percent of teenagers who attempt to kill themselves in that fashion survive the attempt.

Perhaps the main reason that guns are so commonly used in suicide attempts is their widespread availability. Estimates of the number of guns in the United States at the start of 2013 ranged from 250 million to more than 300 million. Estimates of the proportion of U.S. households that owned a firearm ranged from one-third to nearly one-half.

"The doubling in the adolescent suicide rate over the past three decades is largely accounted for by an increase in firearms suicides. This has led to the hypothesis that the increase in the adolescent suicide rate may, in part, be explained by an increase in the availability of firearms to adolescents," said a study published in the *Journal of the American Medical Association.*

An article the summer 2002 *Harvard Public Health Review* explored the question of whether the ready availability of firearms increases the overall number of suicides. Some opponents of gun control argue that if a person is serious about committing suicide, that person will find a way to kill himself or herself if a firearm is not available. The Harvard journal article, however, saw the situation differently.

"A growing body of evidence indicates that . . . where there are more guns, more people are taking their own lives," wrote Dr. Matthew Miller, the associate director of the Harvard Injury Control Center. "For example, American case-control studies all find that a gun in the home is a strong risk factor for suicide, not only for the gun owner, but for other household members as well. The risk of suicide associated with the presence of a firearm in the home is large (an increase of two- to five-fold in most studies), especially when the gun is a handgun or is stored loaded or unlocked.

"A consistent finding across several different types of studies is that the risk of suicide associated with firearms is especially high for adolescents and young adults," continued Miller. "For example, although the suicide rate among adult Americans is similar to that among adults in other developed countries, American children are twice as likely as are their counterparts to commit suicide—a result entirely due to a firearm suicide rate that is ten times higher. Within the U.S. as well, more children commit suicide where there are more guns."

Miller was one of the authors of a 2002 study, published in the Harvard School of Public Health's *Journal of Trauma*, which examined the association between the rate of violent death among 5- to 14-year-olds and the availability of firearms. The study, based on data from 1988 to 1997, compared suicide rates of adolescents in the five states with the highest rates of gun ownership to the suicide rates in the five states with the lowest rates of gun ownership. It concluded that a "statistically significant association exists between gun availability and the rates of unintentional firearm deaths, homicides, and suicides." Miller and his co-authors, Deborah Azrael and David Hemenway, wrote, "The elevated rates of suicide and homicide among children living in states with more guns is not entirely explained by a state's poverty, education, or urbanization and is driven by lethal firearm violence, not by lethal nonfirearm violence."

Of course, many issues can be raised other than the availability of guns to young people who are thinking about suicide. The media regularly reports cases of young children finding access to their parents' weapons and using them as playthings, but with tragic consequences. Some states have tried to curb the availability of guns to young children by passing Child Access Prevention (CAP) laws, which are designed to make gun owners store their weapons in locked cabinets or install trigger locks on their guns, but most states haven't adopted those laws.

According to statistics originally published in the journal *Aggression and Violent Behavior*, a young person in America commits suicide with a firearm every six hours. The suicide rate among young people in the United States is twice as high as the average for other industrialized countries. What's more, there is no difference in the non-firearm suicide rate between the United States and the other industrialized countries. Virtually all the difference is attributable to suicides being committed with guns in America. In 1997, firearms killed no children in Japan, 19 in Great Britain, 57 in Germany, 109 in France, 153 in Canada, and 5,285 in the United States. About 1,400 of those cases in the United States were suicides, while the rest were homicides and accidental shootings. Nearly two-thirds of all suicides committed by teenagers in America are committed with firearms.

It is easy to see why. Guns are efficient. Far fewer people who try to take their own lives survive gunshot wounds than drug overdoses, hangings, and other methods. Says United States Senator Carl Levin, a Michigan Democrat and staunch gun control advocate: "Most gun deaths in America are not the result of murder, but suicide. The numbers are particularly shocking for young people . . . the connection between access to guns and suicide is particularly strong. In fact, the Brady Campaign reports the presence of a gun in the home increases the risk of suicide fivefold."

Suicides are often impulsive acts. People who think about killing themselves also have to decide how to do it. With many methods, there is plenty of time to change one's mind. Suddenly, the act is no longer impulsive. However, firearms don't provide that sort of wiggle room. For the person who pulls the trigger, it is all over in a split-second.

"Adolescent suicide may be a very different phenomenon than suicide among adults, particularly the elderly," reported the 1991 *Journal of the American Medical Association* study. "Elderly people who commit suicide seem to be more likely to have a clear and sustained intent to do so. Young people, on the other hand, are impulsive and not particularly skilled in communication. For them, a suicide attempt may be an attempt to communicate that they are in great pain, although they may be ambivalent about wanting to die. For such adolescents, ready access to a firearm may guarantee that their plea for help will not be heard . . . it can make their self-directed violence fatal and very final."

Child Access Prevention Laws

Proponents of Child Access Prevention laws believe they can go a long way toward preventing suicides in young people and others by taking away the quickest and most effective way of ending life. CAP laws require adults to store loaded guns in a place that is inaccessible to children, such as a locked cabinet, or use a device to lock the gun. Typically, gun owners use locks that are fastened to the trigger or slip into the barrel, making it impossible for the gun to discharge. Under existing CAP laws, adults can face criminal charges if children obtain loaded guns that aren't properly locked or stored.

There is no question that when a person suffering from depression or abusing drugs suddenly becomes irrational, a gun can provide a quick and handy way to end the pain. A study of unintentional and suicidal shootings by children and teens in the Seattle area found that in more than 75 percent of the cases the gun came from either the victim's home or the home of a friend or relative. In other words, only in a minority of the cases was the suicide victim forced to work hard to find a gun.

Florida was the first state to adopt a CAP law, in 1989. Other states that have adopted similar laws include California, Connecticut, Delaware, Florida, Hawaii, Illinois, Iowa, Kansas, Maryland, Massachusetts, Minnesota, Nevada, New Hampshire, New Jersey, North Carolina, Rhode Island, Texas, Virginia, and Wisconsin. In addition, some cities have also enacted local CAP ordinances. In some states, including California, Connecticut, Maryland, Massachusetts, Michigan, New Jersey, New York, Pennsylvania, and Rhode Island, gun stores are required to sell gun locks with the guns.

Other states have resisted any form of CAP legislation. Frequently, gun ownership groups hold a tremendous amount of influence in state capitals and they are often successful in convincing legislators to block gun control measures. Some gun owners, as well as powerful organizations like the National Rifle Association, oppose all forms of gun control, arguing that the Second Amendment to the U.S. Constitution gives them the right to keep guns in their homes.

On the other hand, gun control advocates say there is no arguing with the results. They say statistics show that in the states where CAP laws exist, there are fewer incidents of gun violence involving accidental or suicidal shootings by young people. A 1998 study conducted in Houston showed that the city's CAP ordinance, which had been adopted in 1992, was successful in reducing deaths due to unintentional and suicidal firearm injuries among children under age 16. The study showed that unintentional shooting deaths among children decreased from 21 in the two years before the ordinance went into effect to just one during the four years after the ordinance went into effect.

A Gallup Youth Survey in 1996 indicated that young people support CAP laws and similar measures to control guns. In a survey of 508 teenagers between the ages of 13 and 17, 61 percent of the respondents said they favored stricter gun laws than what were currently in effect. In addition, 54 percent of the young people who participated in the survey said they favored a ban on assault rifles, while 70 percent of the respondents said Americans should not have the right to own large quantities of guns. Finally, only 5 percent of the young people said they owned a gun for self-defense, while 62 percent said they had no intention of owning a gun for the purpose of defending themselves.

Chapter Five

A woman comforts a young girl at the memorial for a friend's suicide. Over the past 40 years, numerous studies have concluded that violence in the entertainment media leads to real-world violence.

Entertainment, the Media, and Suicide

The first time teenage suicide was depicted in the theater was probably in 1595 when William Shakespeare's play *Romeo and Juliet* made its debut. The often-told and often-mimicked story is now quite familiar. Two teenagers defy their families by falling in love; when events and enemies conspire against them, their story ends in tragedy when they take their own lives.

Here are Juliet's last words as she stabs herself after finding the body of her beloved Romeo, who has consumed poison:

What's here? A cup, closed in my true love's hand?
Poison, I see, hath been his timeless end.
O churl, drunk all, and left no friendly drop
To help me after? I will kiss thy lips;
Haply some poison yet doth hang on them,
To make me die with a restorative.
Thy lips are warm!
Yea, noise? Then I'll be brief. O happy dagger!
This is thy sheath. There rest, and let me die.

History does not record whether distraught theater-goers of Shakespeare's era were inspired to commit copycat suicides after seeing *Romeo and Juliet*. In the modern era parents and educators have never been afraid students would be prompted to commit suicide after reading or seeing the play. Still, the violence in the entertainment media today concerns educators, mental health professionals, and parents. Consider these cases that have recently been reported in the news:

In the Russian city of Kstovo, six teenagers were reported to have committed suicide by hanging themselves and jumping from tall buildings. Investigators determined all six victims were devoted fans of the video game Final Fantasy, which includes a depiction of an attempted suicide by one of the characters.

* * *

In Shopiere, Michigan, a 16-year-old boy shot himself in the head while acting out a scene that closely resembled a depiction of Russian roulette in the 1978 film *The Deer Hunter*. Police ruled his death accidental.

* * *

In Ratchaburi, Thailand, a 12-year-old girl hanged herself after playing the video game Bomberman. Authorities speculated that she was frustrated by not achieving a higher score in Bomberman and may have gotten the idea for hanging herself by seeing characters hanged in a popular children's cartoon show on TV. "She loved cartoons," said her mother. "She often said she wanted to vanish like many cartoon characters did."

* * *

Shawn Woolley, 21, was found dead by his mother in his

Wisconsin apartment, the victim of a self-inflicted gunshot wound. Elizabeth Woolley believes her son took his own life after playing the Internet-based role-playing game EverQuest. Shawn Woolley had been diagnosed with depression and a schizoid per-

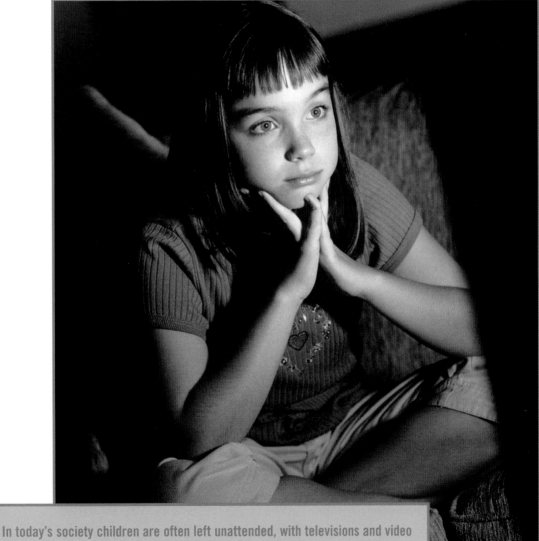

In today's society children are often left unattended, with televisions and video games used as baby sitters from early ages. Exposure to violent content in the media, many experts say, can desensitize young people to violence.

sonality disorder and quit his job a week before his suicide so that he could spend all his time playing EverQuest. Other EverQuest players said they could understand what had driven Woolley over the edge. "To an outsider, it's just like looking at a crack addict — you don't understand how it is until you've been there," said Chris Skinner, who nearly dropped out of college because of his EverQuest habit. "It really is an addiction."

Are these isolated incidents? Hardly. During the past 40 years, there have been more than 1,000 studies on the effects of media violence. While the results are far from conclusive, some of these studies have suggested that violence in the media may lead to an increase in real-world violence.

In 1999, a report to the U.S. Senate Judiciary Committee contained these statistics:

Eighty-seven percent of American households have more than one television, and almost 50 percent of American children have a television set in their rooms. In addition, nearly 89 percent of American homes with children have video game equipment or a personal computer or both.

The average teenager listens to 10,500 hours of rock music between the 7th and 12th grades.

In a typical 18-hour day of television programming, a viewer can observe an average of five violent acts per hour. One study of media violence focused on the programming available on 10 channels, and found 1,846 acts of violence depicted in a single day.

By age 18, the typical American teenager will have seen 200,000 acts of violence on television, including 16,000 simulated murders.

The report did not just focus on television. It cited the increasing reliance on violence in the movies and other forms of entertainment. The report said, "Like television, our cinemas are full of movies that glamorize bloodshed and violence, and one need only listen to popular music and stroll down the aisle of almost any computer store to see that our music and video games are similarly afflicted."

Movies are often violent and depict acts of suicide—even some of Hollywood's most acclaimed films. *The Deer Hunter* earned numerous Academy Awards, including the Oscar for Best Picture of 1978. *It's a Wonderful Life* (1947), which is rerun on television countless times during the Christmas season, is told from the viewpoint of a man considering a suicide attempt. *An Officer and a*

In the beloved Christmas film *It's a Wonderful Life* Jimmy Stewart plays a man who considers suicide when faced with the collapse of his business and other problems.

Gentleman (1982), a blockbuster romance that was very popular among young audiences, depicted a character taking his own life when he failed to measure up to the rigorous standards of a military academy. *The Big Chill* (1983), which examines the baby-boomer generation, opens with a scene of a mortician preparing a suicide victim for burial. *Titanic* (1997), which ranks among the biggest box office hit of all time, included a scene in which one of the major characters attempts suicide. *Titanic* was particularly popular among teenage girls, many of whom reported seeing the movie two or three times. Finally, there have been three Hollywood productions of *Romeo and Juliet* since 1936; the most recent was a hip modern version filmed in 1996 that featured popular young actors Leonardo DiCaprio and Claire Danes in the title roles.

Then there is music. Kurt Cobain and Eminem aren't the only pop stars to have sung about suicide. A big hit for the rapper Ja Rule was titled "Suicide Freedom." MTV refused at first to air the video of heavy metal band Megadeth's song "A Tout Le Monde" because of its depiction of a suicide. The music-oriented cable network finally relented when the producers agreed to include the disclaimer "Suicide is not an answer. Get Help" at the end of the video. The Megadeth song included these lyrics:

> Moving on is a simple thing
> What it leaves behind is hard
> You know the sleeping feel no more pain
> And the living are scarred

The 1999 Senate Judiciary Committee report commented, "A preference for heavy metal music may be a significant marker for alienation, substance abuse, psychiatric disorders, suicide risk, sex-role stereotyping, and risk-taking behaviors during adolescence."

In recent decades, the home entertainment market has been

revolutionized by video games, played either on a television screen or a home computer. A generation ago, when the technology was in its infancy, home video fans could do little more than maneuver electronic paddles across the screen to play a video version of table tennis known as "Pong." Soon, though, even that level of video-game entertainment gave cause for concern. In 1976, a video game that enabled players to score points by running over stick figures was withdrawn from the market after the manufacturer received many complaints about its violent content. Today, such imagery is tame when compared to the mayhem a video game player can whip up on his home screen.

In 2001, researchers at Harvard University studied 55 home video games that had been rated by the industry's self-monitoring system as "E," meaning the content was acceptable for "everyone." The researchers found that 64 percent of the E-rated games involved intentional violence. Said study author Kimberly Thompson: "We didn't expect to see as much violence as we did in some of these games, particularly given their E-rating."

To many researchers, the result of inundating young people with violent entertainment is obvious. They have become desensitized to violence, meaning they don't appreciate violent content for what it truly is. Perhaps there is no clearer example of that than what happened in Littleton, Colorado, in 1999. Eric Harris and Dylan Klebold were fans of the violent video game Doom and programmed the game's playing field to resemble Columbine High School. Harris and Klebold probably pictured themselves acting out a Doom scenario as they traipsed through their high school, mowing down innocent victims. Said the Senate Judiciary Committee report: "Having fed our children death and horror as entertainment, we should not be surprised by the outcome."

The Gallup Youth Survey has been examining the issue of violence in the media for years. The findings are startling, for they show that teenagers have been desensitized to violence but don't realize it.

In 1977, when the Gallup Organization first asked teenagers between the ages of 13 and 17 whether they felt there was too much violence in the movies, 42 percent agreed. A total of 502 American teenagers participated in that poll. In 1999, the Gallup Organization asked the same question of 502 teenagers. This time, 23 percent of the respondents said they thought movies were too violent.

What happened during the 22 years in between? The answer is clear. Teenagers were inundated with thousands and thousands of hours of violence in the cinema, on their television screens, and in video games. Someone who grows up in a world where dramatized or virtual violence has become common may not find stabbings, shootings, or poisonings in movies all that violent.

The Gallup Youth Survey indicated that both boys and girls had been desensitized to violence. In 1977, 35 percent of the boys thought movies were too violent, while in 1999 that number dropped to 20 percent; in 1977, 49 percent of the girls thought movies were too violent, while in 1999 that number dropped to 26 percent.

"Violence is like the nicotine in cigarettes," said David Grossman, a psychologist who testified before the Senate Judiciary Committee. "The reason why the media has to pump ever more violence into us is because we've built up a tolerance. In order to get the same high, we need ever-higher levels. . . . The television industry has gained its market share through an addictive and toxic ingredient."

How the Media Regulates Itself

It is easy to blame the entertainment media, which certainly deserves some of the blame for at least planting the idea of suicide in the heads of some victims. Still, the regulation of violent content in the media is very complex. The U.S. Constitution guarantees

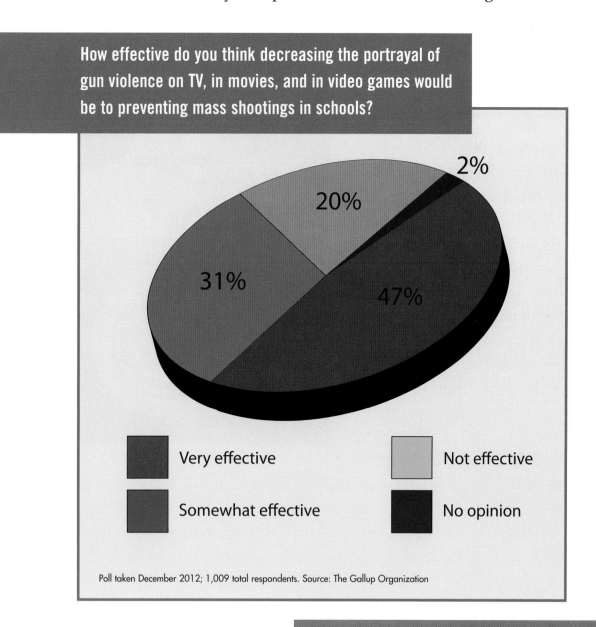

How effective do you think decreasing the portrayal of gun violence on TV, in movies, and in video games would be to preventing mass shootings in schools?

2%

20%

31%

47%

Very effective

Not effective

Somewhat effective

No opinion

Poll taken December 2012; 1,009 total respondents. Source: The Gallup Organization

Nine-year-old Arthur Sawe of Seattle speaks during a 1999 conference held at the White House to examine the marketing of violent media to children. The testimony of Sawe and other young people led the Washington State Retail Association to enforce ratings on violent video games.

freedom of speech and expression, and over the years lawmakers have been very careful not to infringe on the First Amendment rights of writers and artists.

Still, government leaders—presidents, governors, and members of Congress—have at times demanded that the media should act responsibly, and the media has responded.

In 1968, motion picture industry executives developed a film rating system that included the designations "G" for general audiences, "M" for mature, "R" for restricted to viewers over the age of 17 unless accompanied by an adult, and "X" for no one under 17 admitted at all. Over the years, the ratings have undergone several adjustments. Now, the ratings include "G" as well as "PG" for parental guidance advised, "PG-13" for no admission under the age of 13, "R," and "NC-17," which replaced the "X" rating. Films rated "R" carry warning information advising viewers that the movie may include violence, sexual content, depictions of drug use, or other mature content.

The ratings are applied to films by a review board established by the Motion Picture Association of America. There are appeals processes for filmmakers who do not agree with his or her film's ratings. Also, filmmakers are under no requirement to submit the films to the MPAA ratings board, but most do because studios that finance the films usually demand it to comply with public

Hilary Rosen (right), president and CEO of the Recording Industry Association of America, and Jack Valenti, president and CEO of the Motion Picture Association of America, testify before a committee of the House of Representatives, July 2001. The congressional committee was holding a hearing entitled "Media Violence: An Examination of the Entertainment Industry's Efforts to Curb Children's Exposure to Violent Content." A warning label for albums that contain explicit content is displayed with the industry leaders.

sensitivities. The MPAA ratings appear on the advertisements for most films. Theater owners are generally committed to barring admission to anyone not meeting the minimum age guidelines.

Other entertainment media have been slow to copy the ratings system employed by the film industry, but most sectors of the entertainment business eventually found a way to balance the public's desire for responsibility against the constitutional guarantee that artists should be permitted to work in an uncensored environment.

In 1985, the music industry began placing warning labels on records, tapes, and compact discs, advising listeners that song lyrics contained on the albums contained explicit descriptions of violence or sex, or were otherwise unsuitable for young listeners.

The video game industry also adopted a rating system to help guide buyers and advise parents to the nature of the content contained in games. The rating system includes "EC," for games appropriate for players 3 years old and older; "E" for everyone, which means the content is supposed to be suitable for all ages; "KA," which means the content is suitable for "kids to adult," but nevertheless contains some mild violence and mature language; "T" for teen, meaning the content is suitable for players 13 years and older; "M" for mature, which means the game should be played by people 17 years and older because it contains themes of intense violence and language; and "A" for adults only, which means the content includes graphic scenes of sex and violence and is not intended for players under the age of 18.

The television industry has perhaps had the longest struggle to find a way to rate its content. Since the 1990s television executives have imposed a rating system and have agreed to air programming unsuitable for young children late at night, usually in time slots starting after 10 P.M. Also, television programming can be regulated by the V-chip, an electronic device that enables parents to lock out certain content. Most television sets manufactured after January 2000 contain the V-chips.

And so the media has responded somewhat to concerns over the content of the products it provides. Even the media's harshest critics would likely also agree that parents must, in the final analysis, be the people ultimately responsible for the images and sounds that reach the eyes and ears of their teenagers.

Chapter Six

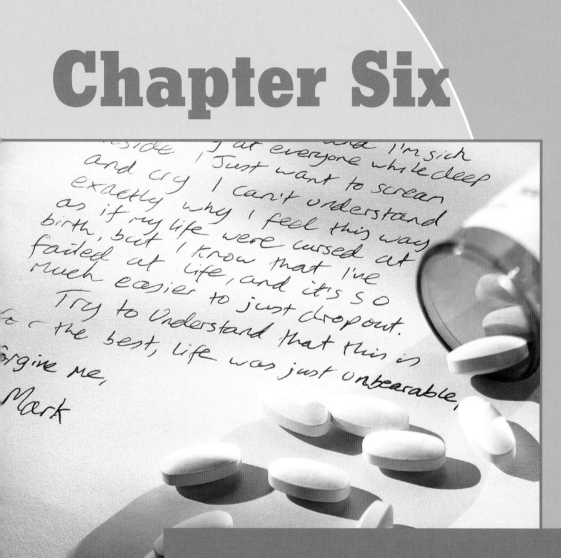

...side ...at everyone while deep ...a I'm sick and cry Just want to scream exactly why I can't understand as if my life were cursed at birth, but I know that I've failed at life, and it's so much easier to just drop out. Try to Understand that this is for the best, life was just unbearable, forgive me, Mark

Drug abuse can be an important contributing factor to teenage suicide. Studies indicate that more than half of adolescents who commit suicide had used drugs or alcohol before their deaths.

Substance Abuse and Suicide

Depression and other forms of mental illness can be a cause of teenage suicide. Violent images in the media may plant the idea. There is no question, though, that the one factor common in most suicides among young people is the abuse of drugs or alcohol.

Throughout the United States the minimum drinking age is 21, and yet many young people have access to alcohol well before they reach that age. They may find beer or wine in their parents' refrigerators, they may have an older friend supply beer, wine or liquor, or they may obtain fake identification cards that enable them to buy alcoholic beverages on their own. As a result, it is no wonder many young people have their first taste of alcohol well before they are legally permitted. It is estimated that in the United States, some 11 million youths under the age of 18 have tasted alcohol, and many of them drink regularly.

Drugs are another matter. Over the years, the

government has made many attempts to stop the use of illegal drugs by young people. Despite the ongoing "war on drugs," marijuana, cocaine, heroin, LSD, and other drugs remain readily available in and around schools throughout the United States. And illegal drugs are only part of the problem. Many young people have access to prescription medications in the possession of older family members or family friends. Such medications, such as tranquilizers and sedatives, often produce some degree of narcotic effect. When researchers talk about drugs abused by young people, prescription medications are included in the count.

Even nonprescription medications can't be ruled out. One study found that 64 percent of young people who tried to take their own lives by overdose made the attempt by using over-the-counter medications available in any pharmacy in America to anyone with the money to buy them.

Studies have concluded there is a definite link between substance abuse and suicide. "Analyses of data for adolescents . . . document a close association between substances and suicide," said a 1989 report on teenage suicide prepared by the U.S. Alcohol, Drug Abuse and Mental Health Administration. "This conclusion is supported by studies of suicidal youth, evaluations of substance abusers and thorough observation of young psychiatric patients."

The study tracked cases involving young suicide victims over a period of 10 years, and concluded that youths who abused drugs and alcohol were up to eight times more likely to kill themselves than youths who didn't drink or take drugs.

The study found "frequent use of nonprescription drugs or alcohol" among 70 percent of the 20 teenagers who committed suicide in the Louisville, Kentucky, area between 1980 and 1983, while almost half the suicide victims between the ages of 15 and

19 in Erie County, New York, had alcohol in their blood. The study also said that in San Diego, California, 75 percent of young suicide victims had abused substances, and that each young victim consumed drugs or alcohol as many as five times just prior to their deaths.

The Link Between Substance Abuse and Suicide

In many cases, depressed or despondent young people turn first to drugs or alcohol as a way of drowning their troubles. They hope that by taking a drink or getting high they will find relief from their anxieties. Of course, this solution does not work. Whatever relief they find is temporary at best. Once the effect of the drink or drug wears off, the old troubles return. Meanwhile, the adolescent has added a new problem to his or her woes—abuse of alcohol and drugs. Perhaps the abuse leads to an addiction, as it did in Kurt Cobain's case. The Alcohol, Drug Abuse and Mental Health Administration report found that 70 percent of teenage suicide victims are heavy users of drugs while 50 percent of young victims have alcohol in their blood at the time of their suicides.

Alcohol and drugs often help make a bad problem worse. Drugs and alcohol—particularly alcohol—often have a depressive effect on the brain. The prescription drug Valium, which is administered to treat anxiety, often has a depressive effect on people. Essentially, drugs and alcohol could make a depressed person feel even worse about himself or herself. Or, they could help alter a person's judgment. As discussed, suicide is an impulsive act. Drugs and alcohol could help make a teenager act impulsively. They interfere with a person's ability to assess risk, make smart choices, and think of solutions to problems.

Some drugs are hallucinogens. LSD (known as "acid") and PCP ("angel dust") may cause their users to hallucinate and totally lose touch with reality while they are under the influence. In some cases, users of hallucinogenic drugs experience violent or suicidal feelings.

Sometimes, young people begin thinking about suicide because of their drug and alcohol problems. When they started drinking and using drugs, they were not suicidal or in any way depressed. They may have been happy, well-adjusted young people who gave in to peer pressure at a party to take a drink or a hit off a marijuana cigarette. Soon, they become regular users and then addicts. Their lives cave in around them. Their school work falls off, they become alienated from their parents and friends, they sink into deep fits of despair as they find themselves unable to shake their habits and straighten out their lives. In the meantime, their drug and alcohol addictions grow worse. Finally, they turn to suicide.

"I remember talking with a desperate young man who was trying to overcome an addiction to heroin," said Paul R. Robbins, a Maryland psychologist and author. "The addiction had unraveled his whole life. He had lost his job, his family, his future. He had become marginalized in society, associating only with other addicts. He was very depressed. I did not have to ask him about suicidal thoughts—he brought them up spontaneously."

Teenage Substance Abuse Statistics

The Gallup Youth Survey has visited the issue of teens and drinking many times over the years. In 1979, 40 percent of boys between the ages of 13 and 17 and 36 percent of girls in that age range reported to occasionally taking a drink behind their parents' backs. That number has fluctuated over the years. In a Gallup Youth Survey poll taken in 2003, 30 percent of the respondents said they "have occasion to use alcoholic beverages." A total of 1,200 teens between the ages of 13 and 17 participated in the 2003 survey.

"Teen drinking is not just a current health problem—it is a predictor of future health problems," said Rick Blizzard, the Gallup Organization's health care consultant. "Chances are that many who develop drinking problems in their teen years will develop other physiological and psychological problems later on."

According to recent studies by the Gallup Youth Survey, about 30 percent of adolescents between the ages of 13 and 17 have tried alcohol, while about 20 percent have used marijuana.

The Gallup Youth Survey has also asked teens about their drug use. In 2002, 20 percent of the respondents to a Gallup Youth Survey reported having used marijuana at least once. The poll queried 501 teenagers between the ages of 13 and 17.

Another issue involving substance abuse and suicide is when drugs are used in the actual commission of the act.

An Oregon study found that girls are more likely than boys to try to take their own lives by taking overdoses of drugs. As discussed, boys are far more likely to try to commit suicide by using firearms and are often successful at their attempts because guns usually don't fail.

But young people often don't understand enough about the drugs they take to know whether the dose is likely to be fatal. The Oregon study found that in nonfatal suicide attempts, 80 percent of the girls and 57 percent of the boys tried to kill themselves through overdoses. In a separate study published in 1992 in the *American Journal of Orthopsychology*, researchers found that in nonfatal suicide attempts involving drug overdoses, 14 percent of the doses taken by the victims were "mild" while 35 percent were "moderate." Essentially, these victims didn't come close to taking doses that were strong enough to do much harm to themselves.

According to the Oregon study, less than 10 percent of all suicide attempts among young people committed through drug overdoses are successful.

Suicide and Prescription Drugs

On the afternoon of January 5, 2002, Charles Bishop, a 15-year-old who was learning how to fly, took off from St. Petersburg-Clearwater International Airport in a four-seat Cessna 172 airplane without his instructor, and without permission from the airport's tower. Bishop first buzzed nearby McDill Air Force Base, then intentionally crashed the stolen aircraft into the 28th floor of a Tampa office building.

This public act of suicide drew national attention, coming just months after the devastating attacks on September 11, 2001, in which terrorists flew hijacked jet planes into the World Trade Center and Pentagon. In a suicide note, Bishop wrote, "Osama bin Laden is absolutely justified in the terror he has caused on 9-11 . . . You will pay—God help you—and I will make you pay!" After a lengthy investigation, in 2003 the National Transportation Safety Board ruled that the crash was caused by "the pilot's unauthorized use of an aircraft for the purpose of committing suicide."

His mother, Julia Bishop, described Charles as "determined to make the world a better place," and said there had been no indication that her son was considering suicide. "This child was a happy, well-balanced, forward-thinking child who had a great deal to live for," she said in a television interview.

Three months after the crash the Bishop family filed a $70 million lawsuit against the drug company Hoffmann-LaRoche, claiming the company's acne medication Accutane had caused Charles Bishop to become psychotic. The drug carries a warning, mandated by the U.S. Food and Drug Administration (FDA), which reads in part, "Accutane may cause depression, psychosis, and, rarely, suicidal ideation, suicide attempts, and suicide." Accutane was also the subject of congressional investigations, brought on by Michigan congressman Bart Stupak, who believed the drug caused his 17-year-old son BJ to kill himself in 2000. "The side effects of Accutane are not worth it," Stupak said.

The drug's defenders—including the manufacturer, psychiatrists, and dermatologists who prescribed Accutane—pointed

In January 2002, 15-year-old Charles Bishop stole a small airplane and crashed it into a Tampa office building. His parents later sued a drug company, claiming that a prescription acne medication caused Bishop to become psychotic.

out that only a couple hundred suicides were ever reported to the FDA, although Accutane was used by more than 13 million people since its introduction in the early 1980s. Also, the FDA itself noted that there was no hard proof of a connection between Accutane and suicide. Nevertheless, the drug's manufacturer removed it from the market in 2009.

Accutane is not the only prescription drug that has been linked to suicide or depression. Many commonly prescribed drugs have side effects. Even drugs intended to treat depression have been linked by some people to suicides or, more commonly, school violence. A survivor of the Columbine shooting—a young man named Mark Taylor, who was shot numerous times by Eric Harris—filed a lawsuit against the drug company Solvay Pharmaceuticals. Solvay manufactures an antidepressant drug, Luvox, that Harris had been taking at the time of the shooting spree. Luvox is in a class of anti-depressant drugs called selective serotonin reuptake inhibitors (SSRI); such well-known drugs as Prozac, Zoloft, and Paxil also are SSRIs. Taylor's lawsuit claimed that the drug made Harris manic and psychotic, causing the rampage.

Chapter Seven

Teenage suicide is a problem that affects young people of all races and family backgrounds. The suicide rate among young African Americans, for example, has increased greatly over the past two decades.

Scared and Alone

One of the few attempts Hollywood has made to film a serious, thoughtful look at teenage suicide was the 1980 movie *Ordinary People*, based on the 1976 novel of the same name by Judith Guest. The book and movie examined the struggles of the Jarrett family, torn by the accidental death of one son and the attempted suicide of another. The movie garnered many Academy Awards, including the Oscar for Best Picture; Timothy Hutton, who played 17-year-old Conrad Jarrett, the suicidal son, won the Oscar as Best Supporting Actor.

Ordinary People brought national attention to the issue of teenage suicide. The only problem with the book and movie, though, is that they make some people think teenage suicide is a problem strictly for the white middle class. The fictional Jarretts are an otherwise successful white family living in a comfortable suburb of Chicago; Calvin, the father, is a tax attorney.

The truth is teenage suicide cuts across economic as well as racial lines. Indeed, more and more young blacks, Hispanics, and members of other minority groups are resorting to suicide. Ironically, one factor believed to be responsible for the rise in the teenage suicide rate among minorities is the ability of their parents to join the middle class. According to the Centers for Disease Control and Prevention, in 1980 the suicide rate among young whites was 157 percent higher than young blacks. In 1998, the CDC reported that while the suicide rate for whites was still higher, it was then just 47 percent higher. "The whole mythology that blacks don't kill themselves needs to be shattered," said psychiatrist Carl Bell.

Over the years, blacks and members of other minority groups have faced social and economic pressures that most whites never had to endure. Racism and poverty have been very much a part of life for blacks, Hispanics, and others in the United States for decades. In the inner cities, minorities have had to cope with drugs, street crime, poor schools, and under-funded social services. Nevertheless, thanks in large part to the Civil Rights legislation of the 1960s, many blacks and other minorities have been able to climb their way into the middle class.

Sociologists expected young blacks and other minority members to excel once they joined the middle class—to become contributing members of society. Certainly, that has occurred. But what came as unexpected news to mental health professionals is that teenagers from minority groups often have as much difficulty adjusting to adolescence as whites, which ultimately means some minority teenagers turn to suicide.

"There's a greater expectation within the African-American community that younger African Americans should be able to do more with the opportunities in front of them," says Sean Joe, a

University of Pennsylvania researcher who authored a study on teenage suicide in the black community.

The CDC found that the suicide rate among blacks between the ages of 10 and 14 increased by a whopping 233 percent between 1980 and 1995. During that same period, the suicide rate among black teenagers between 15 and 19 increased by 126 percent. In that same period, the suicide rate for young whites between 10 and 14 increased by 120 percent, while the rate for older white teenagers increased by 19 percent.

From 1980 to 1995, it is believed that 3,030 black youths committed suicide. During that period, the death rate for young blacks increased from 2.1 deaths to 4.5 deaths per 100,000 persons. The CDC found that 96 percent of the increase in the black teenage suicide rate was caused by firearms. "One of the factors is the easy availability of firearms, especially when suicide is impulsive behavior," said former Surgeon General David Satcher.

The CDC concluded, "Black youths in upwardly mobile families may experience stress associated with their new social environments. Alternately, these youths may adopt coping behaviors of the larger society in which suicide is more commonly used in response to depression and hopelessness."

Young people from other minority groups face similar pressures. A year-long survey conducted in 2001 by the CDC determined that 12 percent of Hispanic students in the 9th through 12th grades had actually taken steps toward ending their own lives. That was much higher than the 9 percent reported among black students, and 8 percent reported among white students. The CDC survey analyzed data submitted by 34 states and 18 cities.

Young Native Americans also have a high suicide rate. A study by officials in New Mexico, which has a large Native American population, found that in 1988 and 1989 the suicide attempt rate for Native Americans between the ages of 15 and 19 was recorded at 60 per 1,000 people. That was much higher than the attempt rate for all New Mexico residents in that age group, which stood at 7 attempts per 1,000 people. New Mexico officials realized they had a suicide epidemic on their hands so they soon introduced intervention programs into the state's Native American community. Those programs had some effect. By 1997, the suicide attempt rate among Native Americans between the ages of 15 and 19 had

SHE WHO WALKS LIKE A LION

The story of Paulette Williams, a young African-American woman from a suburb of Trenton, New Jersey, perhaps best exemplifies the plight of blacks who suddenly find themselves unable to cope in a middle-class world. Born in 1948, she was the daughter of a physician and a teacher. She married early and entered Barnard College in New York, but when she was 19 years old she separated from her husband and found herself falling into a deep depression.

Certainly, her estrangement from her husband contributed to her depression, but she had also been encountering failure as she tried to launch a literary career. A poet, Williams had been sending her work to publishers but finding little but rejection. What's more, at the time women were still struggling for equality in the workplace, and Williams felt herself held back by male-dominated attitudes about what a young woman could accomplish.

And so, Paulette Williams believed she could no longer cope. She tried to kill herself by sticking her head in a gas oven; an aunt discovered her and pulled her out. Still, Williams made subsequent suicide attempts.

"My family life was the all-American dream—privileged, intellectual," she says. "I studied hard, married a lawyer, but my conception of myself was so limited. My daddy told me there were all these things I couldn't do because I was a girl. To be a doctor, a lawyer, a poet—a woman alive. If there had been more respect for my poetry, if I'd been regarded with more care and awareness, my suicide attempts wouldn't have happened. You know, there's a poverty of the spirit we're not always in control of."

dropped to 10 attempts per 1,000 people.

In the United States, gays also regard themselves as members of a minority group. Gay teenagers not only face the pressures of adjusting to adolescence that all teens face, they must also come to terms with their sexuality. Adolescence can be a confusing and awkward time for many teens as they undergo changes in their bodies, learn about dating, and experience their first relationships. A teenager who believes he or she is gay has all of these feelings, as well as others. These might include shame or embarrassment about their desires, or fear of alienation by friends and classmates if they reveal their sexual orientation. As a result, it is not surprising that a New York University School of Medicine study found a high rate of

Williams wrestled with depression and suicide for several more years, but slowly gained control of her life. As a poet, she was able to give voice to her internal struggles. Eventually, she changed her name to Ntozake Shange, which in the African Zulu language means "She Who Walks Like a Lion."

She also found success. In 1976, a series of her poems was adopted to the stage in the Off-Broadway play "For Colored Girls Who Have Considered Suicide/When the Rainbow is Enuf." The play, which consisted of seven black actresses reciting Shange's verse in choreographed monologues, became a genuine hit and earned an Obie Award, an honor bestowed on the Off-Broadway theater.

The play attempts to capture the experience of the young and poor African-American woman in the United States. For many young inner-city black women, that experience includes rape, abortion, abandonment, single parenthood, drugs and despair. Certainly, as the title suggests, suicide is part of that experience.

"There are certain kinds of emotional pain that make me feel horrible," says Shange. "I ache. I feel like I have these terrible hot rods in my arm. When I'm in that particular pain and despair I don't have any hope, any sense of the morning. I want to get out of my body. Like in my poem, which says I want to jump right out of my bones and be done with myself. I meant that. Death could not be worse."

attempted suicide in the teenage gay community. The 2001 study of New York State teens in the 7th through 12th grades found that 28 percent of males and 21 percent of females who identified themselves as gay had reported attempting suicide.

An earlier study conducted by the U.S. Alcohol, Drug Abuse and Mental Health Administration also reported a high suicide rate among gay teens, finding that young gay and lesbian people are confused and traumatized by society's attitudes toward homosexuality.

"No group of people are more strongly affected by the attitudes and conduct of society than are the young," said the study. "Gay and lesbian youth are strongly affected by the negative attitudes and hostile responses of society to homosexuality. The resulting poor self-esteem, depression, and fear can be a fatal blow to a fragile identity. Two ways that society influences suicidal behavior by gay and lesbian youth are the ongoing discrimination against and the oppression of homosexuals, and the portrayal of homosexuals as self-destructive."

In 1998, the Gallup Youth Survey found that most young people had a tolerant or supportive attitude toward homosexuals. In its survey of 500 teens between the ages of 13 and 17, 82 percent said gays should be treated equally in the workplace while 80 percent said health benefits should be extended to the partners of gay employees. A total of 73 percent said gays should have the right to join the armed forces while 64 percent thought they should be able to adopt children.

And yet, many young gays are still made to feel like outcasts. The Washington-based National Gay and Lesbian Task Force estimated that by the late 1990s, no fewer than 49 proposals to deny rights to gays and lesbians were making their way through state legislatures. Eighteen states sought to ban gay marriages.

Some of the legislative efforts were aimed directly at gay teens. For example, Utah took the dramatic step of barring all extra-curricular clubs at schools rather than permit alliances of gay and lesbian students to meet on school grounds. In 1999, anti-gay groups in Oregon circulated petitions seeking to bar discussion of gay and lesbian issues in classrooms.

Supporters of gay rights see a direct connection between discrimination against gays and the suicide rate among gay and lesbian young people. "Gay and lesbian teenagers are killing themselves in staggering numbers," reported *The Advocate*, a gay-rights magazine. "They are hanging themselves in high school classrooms, jumping from bridges, shooting themselves on church altars, cutting themselves with razor blades, and downing lethal numbers of pills. A conservatively estimated 1,500 young gay and lesbian lives are terminated every year because these troubled youths have nowhere to turn. They are scared and alone."

The rate of suicide is high among gay and lesbian teens. In a 2001 study of adolescents in seventh through twelfth grades who identified themselves as homosexual, 28 percent of males and 21 percent of females reported attempting suicide.

Chapter Eight

Most teenagers in the United States do not suffer from depression or consider ending their lives. However, that does not make the problem of teenage suicide any less real or important.

Attached to Life

The statistics, case studies, and trends cited in this book are troubling. They present an impression that young people in the United States are profoundly depressed and live angst-ridden existences, exposed to media violence and clouded by drug and alcohol abuse. But that is not true; only a very small percentage of teenagers go through with their suicide plans. Most teenagers are well-adjusted, intelligent, and capable of making the right decisions.

The Gallup Youth Survey looked at teen attitudes in several different ways over the years. For the most part, participants in those surveys were generally upbeat about the future and anxious to become contributing members of society. In 2001, for example, 99 percent of teenagers responding to the Gallup Youth Survey said they had plans for themselves following completion of high school. The poll showed 87 percent planned to go to college, 4 percent planned to look for full-time

employment, and 8 percent planned to join the armed services.

A Gallup Youth Survey conducted in 2000 found that 87 percent of young people were "satisfied with the way things are going in their personal lives." In addition, 93 percent of the teens said life was treating them "fairly or very fairly" while 86 percent said they were "totally fulfilled or somewhat fulfilled."

Troubles at home are often cited as reasons for teenage suicide. The fact is, however, that most teens do not have troubles at home. Another Gallup Youth Survey poll taken in 2000 reported that 97 percent of the respondents got along with their parents either "fairly well" or "very well."

Finally, teenagers see themselves as the hope for the future. A

1999 poll by the Gallup Youth Survey reported that 73 percent of young people who participated saw themselves as helping to shape "a new hope and sense of purpose for our world."

Those statistics are heart-warming and provide optimism that teenage suicide is a problem that can be licked. Indeed, there are many ways the problem is being attacked.

HOW TO HELP

What should you do if you suspect a friend intends to commit suicide? According to the American Association of Suicidology, here are some ways to help:

- Be direct. Talk openly and matter-of-factly about suicide.

- Be willing to listen. Express your feelings and encourage your friend to express his or her feelings.

- Don't be judgmental. Don't debate whether suicide is right or wrong.

- Don't lecture your friend on the value of life.

- Become available to your friend and let him or her know you want to become involved. Show interest and support.

- Don't dare your friend to commit suicide.

- Don't act shocked. That could help create a distance between you and your friend.

- Don't promise to keep your friend's plans secret. Involve others. Seek support.

- Don't offer false reassurances that everything will work itself out. You may come off seeming shallow. Instead, talk over alternatives and promise to help your friend find sensible ways to address his or her problems.

- Take action. If you know your friend has access to a gun in the house, have it removed or locked up. If you know your friend has stockpiled pills, take them away.

- Seek professional help. Most schools have counselors trained as suicide watchdogs. Police departments are good places to call as well. Many cities and counties have human services agencies that will intervene.

For example, the Centers for Disease Control regularly assesses the responses by state and local governments and school districts to health issues that affect young people, including suicide. An assessment by the CDC in 2011 found that about 70 percent of all high schools in the United States offered a "Student Assistance Program" to students. The programs provide professional help to students who are experiencing the type of personal and social problems that would prompt them to consider suicide. In nearly

SURVIVORS OF SUICIDE

Adolescent suicide victims leave behind grieving parents, brothers, sisters, and friends. Often, the survivors feel an overwhelming sense of guilt because they failed to prevent the suicide. They need help, too.

The American Association of Suicidology estimates that for every suicide, there are six survivors. That means some 12,000 people a year are left behind by adolescent suicide victims.

There are places for these survivors to obtain grief counseling. Support groups for suicide survivors can be found in most communities. Usually, they meet in churches, hospitals, and municipal buildings. A person trained in grief counseling often serves as facilitator. Participants are encouraged to talk about their grief. For survivors, there is often comfort in being able to talk about grief with others who have also survived suicides.

Friends of suicide survivors are very important to their therapy. In many cases suicide survivors find it hard to lean on other family members because they are, after all, overcoming the pain of suicide themselves. So if you have a friend who is a survivor of a suicide, you may be the one person that survivor can turn to for help.

half those programs, schools have made either one-on-one counseling or small-group discussions available to young people at risk. In addition, more than a third of the school districts in the United States have contracted with outside mental health agencies to provide suicide intervention programs. The CDC also found that 75 percent of all senior high schools in the United States provide some level of suicide prevention education.

There is no question that a stable home life can be a deterrent to suicide. Sadly, stability is often lacking in many American homes. A May 2001 Gallup Youth Survey reported that just 59 per-

Just your physical presence and willingness to listen can help in the healing process. Allow survivors to tell you their feelings, but don't push them. Don't give them shallow answers such as "I know how you feel" because chances are you don't. Also, comments like "Time heals all wounds" or "Think of what you still have to be thankful for" don't help, either. And don't try to explain the victim's motivations or write off the victim as insane or crazy—the victim was your friend's close family member. Those who are left behind after a suicide need help finding their own answers.

Be patient—grief takes a long time to overcome. Don't be afraid to use the name of the victim when talking to his or her survivors. Hearing the name can be comforting and it confirms that you haven't forgotten the victim, who was a very important person in your friend's life. Make a special effort to be there for survivors during holidays or on the anniversary of the victim's death.

"Grief following suicide is always complex," says Dr. Alan D. Wolfelt, a physician and director of the Center for Loss and Life Transition in Fort Collins, Colorado. "Survivors don't 'get over it.' Instead, with support and understanding they can come to reconcile themselves to its reality. Don't be surprised by the intensity of their feelings. Sometimes, when they least suspect it, they may be overwhelmed by feelings of grief. Accept that survivors may be struggling with explosive emotions, guilt, fear and shame, well beyond the limits experienced in other types of deaths. Be patient, compassionate and understanding."

Although the pressures teenagers feel can seem insurmountable, family members and friends can form an invaluable support network, helping young people deal with the many crises of adolescence.

cent of the teens between the ages of 13 and 17 who responded to the poll lived with both parents.

Many mental health professionals believe that educators can prevent suicides by getting their students interested and involved in classroom activities and by empowering them to achieve goals they never believed they had the ability to achieve. Young people who learn they are capable of accomplishing great things generally do not look for reasons to kill themselves.

Getting young people involved in school projects as well as activities away from school are also regarded as important deterrents to teen suicide. After all, many potential suicide victims feel alienated from the mainstream. They are loners who believe nobody cares about them. Making them part of a team helps them feel they belong and their life has a purpose.

This is not a new concept. The French sociologist Emile Durkheim first wrote about the relationship between a strong society and mental health in 1897 in a book he titled *Suicide*. When society offers too little guidance, Durkheim wrote, the individual feels alienated and the risk of suicide increases. "When society is strongly integrated, it holds individuals under its control, considers them at its service and thus forbids them to dispose willfully of themselves," he wrote. Members of a society, Durkheim said, "cling to life more resolutely when belonging to a group they love, so as not to betray interests they put before their own. The bond that unites them with the common cause attaches them to life."

Glossary

ANXIETY—a mental condition that causes its sufferers to feel powerless to cope with threatening events, often accompanied by such physical effects as sweating and trembling.

ATTENTION DEFICIT DISORDER—believed to be caused by a chemical imbalance in the brain, ADD sufferers have short attention spans and exhibit impulsive behavior. Also known as hyperactivity.

BULIMIA NERVOSA—a serious eating disorder characterized by compulsive overeating (binging) followed by self-induced vomiting or laxative use (purging), and often accompanied by feelings of guilt or depression.

DEPRESSION—an emotional condition characterized by feelings of sadness, hopelessness and inadequacy.

DOCTOR-ASSISTED SUICIDE—an illegal practice in which a physician helps a person to end his or her life.

EUPHORIA—a general feeling of happiness.

LSD—abbreviation for lysergic acid diethylamide, an illegally-manufactured drug that produces hallucinations and delusions in its users. Also known as "acid."

MELANCHOLY—general state of sadness or depression.

NEUROTIC—state of suffering from a variety of mental disorders, including anxiety and depression.

PCP—abbreviation for phencyclidine, a drug developed in the 1950s as an intravenous anesthetic but discontinued in 1965 because it causes patients to become agitated, disoriented and delusional.

PSYCHIATRIST—a physician who specializes in treating mental illness.

PSYCHOLOGIST—a researcher, educator, or counselor who studies and treats human behavior.

Glossary

PURGING—in bulimia nervosa, the act of ridding the body of food either through forced vomiting or the use of laxatives.

SCHIZOID—a personality type that suggests schizophrenia.

SCHIZOPHRENIA—a mental illness that causes delusions or hallucinations, or causes the sufferer to have a distorted view of reality, a fragmented personality, or expressions of other forms of bizarre behavior.

SEDATIVE—medication that reduces excitement, nervousness, or irritation.

SEMIAUTOMATIC—when referring to firearms, a weapon that is mechanically capable of reloading itself but requires the user to squeeze the trigger to fire off each round of ammunition. An automatic weapon discharges many shots with each squeeze of the trigger.

SEROTONIN—a neurotransmitter found in the brain that has a great effect on human moods and behaviors.

SUICIDE CONTAGION—a situation in which a suicide leads to an increase in other cases of suicide.

TRANQUILIZER—medication administered to control anxiety and other mental disorders.

Further Reading

Bornstein, Kate. *Hello Cruel World: 101 Alternatives to Suicide for Teens, Freaks, and Other Outlaws*. New York: Seven Stories Press, 2006.

Bender, David L. and Bruno Leone, editors. *Suicide: Opposing Viewpoints*. San Diego: Greenhaven Press, 1992.

Cobain, Bev. *When Nothing Matters Anymore: A Survival Guide for Depressed Teens*. Minneapolis: Free Spirit Publishing, 2007.

Henderson, Kathy Harris. *A Brief Guide to Teen Suicide Prevention*. New York: Searchlight Press, 2012.

Heckler, Richard A. *Waking Up Alive: The Descent, the Suicide Attempt and the Return to Life*. New York: G.P. Putnam's Sons, 1994.

Huddle, Lorena, and Jay Schleifer. *Teen Suicide*. New York: Rosen, 2011.

Lester, David. *The Enigma of Adolescent Suicide*. Philadelphia: The Charles Press, 1993.

Portner, Jessica. *One in Thirteen*. Beltsville, Md.: Robins Lane Press, 2001.

Robbins, Paul R. *Adolescent Suicide*. Jefferson, N.C.: McFarland and Company Publishers, 1998.

Internet Resources

http://www.gallup.com
The Gallup Organization's World Wide Web pages feature information on the Gallup Youth Surveys as well as the other polling work conducted by the organization.

http://www.cdc.gov
The Centers for Disease Control makes available dozens of studies and articles about suicide causes, trends, and treatments on its Internet site.

http://www.nimh.nih.gov
The National Institute of Mental Health coordinates the federal government's efforts to study and treat mental illnesses in the United States. NIMH's Internet site includes many articles and sources of information on teenagers and suicide.

http://www.mentalhealthamerica.net
Mental Health America (formerly the National Mental Health Association) is a nonprofit organization dedicated to helping all people live mentally healthier lives.

http://www.pbs.org/thesilentepidemic
Companion World Wide Web site to the PBS documentary "The Silent Epidemic," which explored teenage suicide. The documentary includes interviews with teenagers who survived suicide attempts.

Internet Resources

http://www.bradycampaign.org

Internet address of the Brady Campaign, the Washington-based lobbying organization that advocates gun-control measures. The site includes facts, essays, and publications that support its arguments.

http://www.suicidology.org

World Wide Web site of the American Association of Suicidology. The site contains information on prevention of suicides as well as treatment options for potential victims. There is also information for survivors, support groups, and crisis centers, as well as dozens of links to other suicide-related Internet sites.

http://www.afsp.org

The Internet page maintained by the American Foundation of Suicide Prevention contains a state by state directory of support groups for suicide survivors. Visitors can find contacts, phone numbers, and meeting dates for dozens of survivor support groups in the United States.

Index

Accutane, 83–84, 85
 See also prescription medication
African Americans, *86*, 88–89, *90–91*
Aggression and Violent Behavior, 54–55
alcohol, 29–30, 77, 79–80, 81
 See also substance abuse
Allen, Jamie, 35
American Association of Suicidology, *97*, *98*
 See also prevention
American College Health Association, 25
American Journal of Orthopsychology, 82
anorexia nervosa, 42–43
anti-depressant medication, *46*, 47
 See also prescription medication
assisted suicide, *26–27*
Attention Deficit Disorder, 37
Azrael, Deborah, 54

Beerer, James, 21
Bell, Carl, 88
The Big Chill, 68
bipolar disorder (manic depression), 28, 36–41
 See also mental illness
Bishop, Charles, 82–83, *84*
Blizzard, Rick, 13, 81
Bomberman (video game), 64
Brady, James, 48, *49*
 Brady, Sarah, *49*
Brady Center to Prevent Gun Violence, 52, 57, *60*
 See also Brady Law
Brady Law, 48–49
 See also firearms
Breivik, Anders, 48
Brown, Randy, 48
bulimia nervosa, 42–43

CAP laws. *See* Child Access Prevention (CAP) laws
Carroll, Michael, 9, 11
Child Access Prevention (CAP) laws, 54, 57–60
 See also firearms
Cho, Seung-Hui, 47–48, 49–50
Cobain, Beverly, 37–38
Cobain, Frances, 36
Cobain, Kurt, 28, *32*, 33–36, 37–38, 68, 79
college students, 25–28
Columbine High School, *44*, 45–48, 49–51, *56*, 69, 85

Danes, Claire, 68
Davies, Kaylieh, *13*
Davies, Martin, *13*
The Deer Hunter, 64, 67
Delahanty, Thomas, 49
depression, 22–23, 24, *26*, 28, 30, 37–42, 43, 65, 77
 See also mental illness
DiCaprio, Leonardo, 68
divorce. *See* home life
Doom (video game), 69
drinking. *See* alcohol
drug overdoses, 51, 52, 57, 78, 82
drugs, 19, 77–78, 79–80, 81–82
 See also substance abuse
Duran, Philip, 51
 See also Columbine High School
Durkheim, Emile, 101
dysthymia, 41
 See also depression

eating disorders, 42–43

Numbers in **bold italic** refer to captions and graphs.

Index

elderly people, 24, **25**, 57
Eminem, 11, **12–13**, 68
EverQuest (video game), 65–66

failed suicide attempts, 16–17, 52
family history, 15, 28–29, 33, 38
Fawcett, Jan, 23
Ferdock, Dan, 19–20, 21, 22
Final Fantasy (video game), 64
firearms, 16, 53–54, 82, 89
    and Child Access Prevention (CAP)
        laws, 54, 57–60
    and Columbine High School,
        48–51
    and gun control laws, **50**, 52, **59**,
        61
    as primary method of committing
        suicide, 51–52, **53**, 54–57
freedom of speech, 71–72, 74
    See also media violence

Gallup Youth Survey
    awareness of suicide, **10**, 11–12
    eating disorders, 43
    gun control laws, 61
    home life, 96, 100
    media violence, 70
    risky behavior of teens, 34
    school violence, **56**
    sexual orientation, 92
    substance abuse, 80–82
    suicide thoughts, 14
    teen attitudes, 95–97
        See also polls
gays. See sexual orientation
gender differences, 14, 16, 17, 24, **25**,
    31, 51, 82
Generation X, 34, 35
genetic factors. See family history
Goodwin, Fred, 84

Grossman, David, 70
gun shows, 49, 50–51
    See also firearms
guns. See firearms

Harris, Eric, 45–51, **56**, 69, 85
Harvard Public Health Review, 52–53
hate groups, **56**
Hawkins, Robert, 48, 49
Heckler, Richard A., 17
Hemenway, David, 54
Hispanics, 88, 89
    See also race
home life, 25, **29,** 96, 99–100
homosexuality. See sexual orientation
Houston, Texas, 60
Hurcombe, David, 9, 11, **13**, 15–16

impulse behavior, 30–31
It's a Wonderful Life, 67

Ja Rule, 68
Joe, Sean, 88–89
Journal of Nervous and Mental Disease,
    42
*Journal of the American Medical
    Association*, 52, 57
Journal of Trauma, 54

Kevorkian, Jack, **26–27**
Klebold, Dylan, 45–48, 50–51, **56**, 69

Landis, Marc, 19–20, 21, 22
Lanza, Adam, 48, 49, 50
Levin, Carl, 57
Littleton, Colorado, 45, 69
    See also Columbine High School
Louisville, Kentucky, 78
Love, Courtney, 36
    See also Cobain, Kurt

Index

Index

Picture Credits

Contributors

GEORGE GALLUP JR. (1930–2011) was involved with The Gallup Organization for more than 50 years. He served as chairman of The George H. Gallup International Institute and served on many boards involved with health, education, and religion, including the Princeton Religion Research Center, which he co-founded.

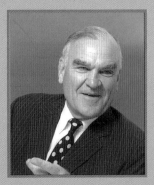

Mr. Gallup was internationally recognized for his research and study on youth, health, religion, and urban problems. He wrote numerous books, including *My Kids On Drugs?* with Art Linkletter (Standard, 1981); *The Great American Success Story* with Alec Gallup and William Proctor (Dow Jones-Irwin, 1986); *Growing Up Scared in America* with Wendy Plump (Morehouse, 1995); *Surveying the Religious Landscape: Trends in U.S. Beliefs* with D. Michael Lindsay (Morehouse, 1999); and *The Next American Spirituality* with Timothy Jones (Chariot Victor Publishing, 2002).

Mr. Gallup received his BA degree from the Princeton University Department of Religion in 1954, and held seven honorary degrees. He received many awards, including the Charles E. Wilson Award in 1994, the Judge Issacs Lifetime Achievement Award in 1996, and the Bethune-DuBois Institute Award in 2000. Mr. Gallup passed away in November 2011.

THE GALLUP YOUTH SURVEY was founded in 1977 by Dr. George Gallup to provide ongoing information on the opinions, beliefs and activities of America's high school students and to help society meet its responsibility to youth. The topics examined by the Gallup Youth Survey have covered a wide range—from abortion to zoology. From its founding through the year 2001, the Gallup Youth Survey sent more than 1,200 weekly reports to the Associated Press, to be distributed to newspapers around the nation.

HAL MARCOVITZ is a Pennsylvania-based journalist. He has written more than 50 books for young readers. His other titles for the Gallup Youth Survey series include *Teens and Career Choices* and *Teens and Volunteerism*. He lives in Chalfont, Pennsylvania, with his wife, Gail, and daughters Ashley and Michelle.